# Jump Start Vue.js

- **Product Manager:** Simon Mackie
- **Technical Editor:** James Hibbard
- **English Editor:** Ralph Mason
- **Cover Designer:** Alex Walker

Published by SitePoint Pty. Ltd.

48 Cambridge Street Collingwood

VIC Australia 3066

Web: www.sitepoint.com

Email: books@sitepoint.com

ISBN 978-1-925836-09-7 (print)

ISBN 978-1-925836-25-7 (ebook)

## About Nilson Jacques

Nilson is a software developer from England with a passion for learning, using, and writing about the Web. In his spare time he enjoys spending time with his family, playing the guitar, and reading.

## About SitePoint

SitePoint specializes in publishing fun, practical, and easy-to-understand content for web professionals. Visit https://www.sitepoint.com/ to access our blogs, books, newsletters, articles, and community forums. You'll find a stack of information on JavaScript, PHP, Ruby, mobile development, design, and more.

# Table of Contents

# Preface

"Why should I be learning Vue in 2019?" you might be asking. A lot of people assume that React has the market for JavaScript client-side frameworks sewn up, but I strongly believe that this year will continue to see Vue.js make great in-roads into that market.

Vue continues to win over developers with its approachable learning curve, powerful feature-set, and fantastic documentation. Much in the same way that Ruby on Rails won converts from other languages with its focus on the developer experience, many prefer Vue's simplicity and 'batteries included' approach over frameworks like React and Angular.

With version 3.0 due for release this year, promising performance improvements, falling file sizes, and better TypeScript support, 2019 is looking to be another great year for Vue.js. There's never been a better time to start learning the library and its ecosystem!

## Who Should Read This Book?

This books is for developers with experience of JavaScript. If you've already used a component-based framework such as React, you'll find this book an easy read, but it's also suitable for readers with no prior experience of such frameworks.

## Conventions Used

You'll notice that we've used certain typographic and layout styles throughout this book to signify different types of information. Look out for the following items.

### Code Samples

Code in this book is displayed using a fixed-width font, like so:

```
<h1>A Perfect Summer's Day</h1>
<p>It was a lovely day for a walk in the park.
The birds were singing and the kids were all back at school.</p>
```

Where existing code is required for context, rather than repeat all of it, ⋮ will be displayed:

```
function animate() {
  ⋮
new_variable = "Hello";
}
```

- Some lines of code should be entered on one line, but we've had to wrap them because of page constraints. An ↪ indicates a line break that exists for formatting purposes only, and should be ignored:

```
URL.open("https://www.sitepoint.com/responsive-web-
↪design-real-user-testing/?responsive1");
```

## Tips, Notes, and Warnings

### Hey, You!

Tips provide helpful little pointers.

### Ahem, Excuse Me ...

Notes are useful asides that are related—but not critical—to the topic at hand. Think of them as extra tidbits of information.

### Make Sure You Always ...

... pay attention to these important points.

### Watch Out!

Warnings highlight any gotchas that are likely to trip you up along the way.

# Supplementary Materials

- https://github.com/spbooks/jsvuejs1 is the book's code archive, which contains code examples found in the book.
- https://www.sitepoint.com/community/ are SitePoint's forums, for help on any tricky problems.
- **books@sitepoint.com** is our email address, should you need to contact us to report a problem, or for any other reason.

Chapter

# Vue.js: the Basics

# 1

Since Facebook introduced React in 2013, component-based UI frameworks have become increasingly popular. They allow you to build your applications as collections of self-contained, reusable components that can manage their own state and can be declaratively composed into more complex interfaces.

The second generation of Google's Angular framework is based around the component paradigm, and a number of smaller, light-weight libraries such as HyperApp have cropped up in recent years.

Amidst this seemingly ever-growing collection of frameworks and libraries came Vue.js (referred to simply as Vue, from here on). Released in 2014, Vue was created by a Google engineer called Evan You, who was inspired to create it after having worked with AngularJS.

Vue has seen a meteoric rise in popularity and is now considered one of the main front-end frameworks, and not without good reason. It was designed to be flexible and easy to adopt, making it just as easy to integrate into projects and use alongside non-Vue code as it is to build complex client-side applications.

## Why Choose Vue?

If you're reading this, you've already decided that Vue is worth a look, but there are plenty of good reasons to choose it for your next project.

- **It's easy to "sprinkle onto" an existing site**. You can start using Vue on existing websites without having to implement a build step and introduce a new setup and tooling to your workflow. In fact, Vue is the perfect go-to tool for many situations where you'd previously have reached for jQuery!

- **Vue's component-based architecture**. Of course, Vue is also more than capable of building modern single page applications (SPAs), allowing you to develop your apps as modular, reusable components.

- **Its comprehensive ecosystem**. Pre-built components for almost every conceivable use are available from Vue's large community of developers. On top of that, popular libraries exist to provide common functionality such as client-side routing, state management, and server-side rendering! Many of these are also maintained by the official Vue team, in contrast to React, where there aren't always official solutions available.

**It's widely used**. Vue is being used by a diverse range of businesses, from GitLab to the Chinese giant Alibaba. It's also been adopted by the PHP framework Laravel as its default library for building client-side apps. It's safe to say that these organizations consider Vue to be a sensible choice with good future prospects. Its popularity also means that it's easy to get help with your problems on various support sites and forums.

## Getting Started

In order to get to know Vue and see how it works, let's walk through the basics. To get a feel for what we can do with the framework, we're going to start with a static HTML page and add in some basic interactivity with Vue.

## Staff Directory

| Avatar | First Name | Last Name | Email | Phone | Department |
|--------|-----------|-----------|-------|-------|-----------|
| | amelia | austin | amelia.austin@example.com | (651)-507-3705 | Engineering |
| | bobbie | murphy | bobbie.murphy@example.com | (925)-667-7604 | Management |
| | brandon | griffin | brandon.griffin@example.com | (509)-317-9506 | Management |
| | kristin | terry | kristin.terry@example.com | (021)-544-1184 | Sales |
| | tammy | gibson | tammy.gibson@example.com | (815)-727-0663 | Support |

1-1. A basic staff directory

As an example, we're going to use this fictional employee directory, which you can find online as a **CodeSandbox**[1].

## The Vue Instance

Let's start by loading the Vue library from a CDN. For simple use cases, like adding some interactivity to existing websites, this will get us up and running quickly without having to introduce a build step:

```
<script src="https://cdn.jsdelivr.net/npm/vue@2.5.17/dist/vue.js"></script>
```

 **Development vs Production**

We're including the development version, which outputs helpful warnings in the console to help you avoid common pitfalls, and integrates with the Vue devtools (which we'll cover later). In production, you'll want to switch to the minimized version `vue.min.js`, which is ~30KB gzipped.

Next, we need to create a new Vue instance:

```
new Vue({
  el: "#main"
});
```

So far, all we've done is told Vue that we want this instance to manage an area of the DOM defined by the selector `#main`. It will use this area of the page as a template.

It will parse this chunk of HTML, looking for expressions that are part of the template language (which we'll look at shortly) and binding them to our instance data where applicable.

## Reactive Data

To be able to do something useful with our Vue instance, we need to give it some

---

1. https://codesandbox.io/s/wnzrwy33y7

data. We do this by defining a key called *data* whose property is an object containing all the data we want Vue to work with.

Any values that are assigned to the *data* object (including nested objects and arrays) become **reactive**, meaning that Vue will observe them and automatically re-render the UI *when they change.*

Let's add some example data to our instance:

```
new Vue({
  el: "#main",
  data: {
    heading: "Staff Directory",
    employees: [
      {
        "firstName": "amelia",
        "lastName": "austin",
        "photoUrl": "https://randomuser.me/api/portraits/thumb/women/9.jpg",
        "email": "amelia.austin@example.com",
        "phone": "(651)-507-3705",
        "department": "Engineering"
      },
      {
        "firstName": "bobbie",
        "lastName": "murphy",
        "photoUrl": "https://randomuser.me/api/portraits/thumb/women/79.jpg",
        "email": "bobbie.murphy@example.com",
        "phone": "(925)-667-7604",
        "department": "Management"
      }
    ]
  }
});
```

**Always Declare Your Data Properties**

It may be that some of the data you want to work with won't be available to your instance when you initialize it (for example, if it's loaded via an Ajax request). Vue requires you to declare all root-level keys up front, as they can't be added dynamically later on.

It's good practice to declare default values anyway, as you won't run into errors trying to access non-existent properties, and it helps to document the data structure of your instance (or component, as we'll see later).

At this stage, our instance has all the data it needs, but it won't be able to render anything without a template. Let's look at how to create one next.

## Template Syntax

So now we have our Vue instance, we've given it some data, and we've told it which part of the page it should be looking at for its template. How do we render our data?

### Interpolations

To output primitive values from our instance data, such as numbers and strings, we use the curly brace syntax (aka the Mustache syntax):

```
<h1 class="ui center aligned header">{{ heading }}</h1>
```

You can also use any valid JavaScript statement between double braces, which Vue will evaluate before rendering.

### Code

```
<div id="app">
  <p>The price is: {{ price * 1.20 }} (inc. VAT)</p>
```

```
  </div>
  <script>
    new Vue({
      el: '#app',
      data: {
        price: 25
      }
    });
  </script>
```

**Output**

```
The price is: £30 (inc. VAT)
```

In this example, we're performing a calculation with the data *price* before outputting it. The calculation is just a normal JavaScript expression.

## Directives

Of course, to build any sort of interesting UI, we need to do more than just display simple values. Vue's template syntax includes directives for looping and conditional display logic, as well as binding HTML attributes to reactive data properties. Directives are attributes you add to DOM elements and components (very similar to AngularJS's ng-* directives).

### v-for

Thinking back to our example instance data, you probably already wondered how we go about looping over collections of data such as arrays. The *v-for* directive allows us to tell Vue that we want a section of our template to be rendered for every item in a collection (which can be an array *or* an object):

```
<tbody>
  <tr v-for="employee in employees">
    <td>
      <img src="https://randomuser.me/api/portraits/thumb/women/9.jpg"
           class="ui mini rounded image" />
```

```
    </td>
    <td>{{ employee.firstName }}</td>
    <td>{{ employee.lastName }}</td>
    <td>{{ employee.email }}</td>
    <td>{{ employee.phone }}</td>
    <td>{{ employee.department }}</td>
  </tr>
</tbody>
```

Here, the `tr` element with the `v-for` directive, and all its child elements, will be repeated for each employee in the array. You might be wondering why the image `src` is hard-coded here. We have to use a different method for binding data to attributes, as we'll see shortly.

## Staff Directory

| Avatar | First Name | Last Name | Email | Phone | Department |
|--------|-----------|-----------|-------|-------|------------|
| | amelia | austin | amelia.austin@example.com | (651)-507-3705 | Engineering |
| | bobbie | murphy | bobbie.murphy@example.com | (925)-667-7604 | Management |
| | kristin | terry | kristin.terry@example.com | (021)-544-1184 | Sales |
| | brandon | griffin | brandon.griffin@example.com | (509)-317-9506 | Management |
| | tammy | gibson | tammy.gibson@example.com | (815)-727-0663 | Support |

1-2. The effect of applying v-for

As with React, when rendering a list in Vue it's strongly recommended that you give the repeated elements a unique value as a key. This helps Vue to optimize rendering when adding and removing elements from the collection. You can specify a key using the special `:key` directive on the element that is to be repeated:

```
<tr v-for="user in users" :key="user.id>
```

 **Using an Array Index as a Key**

If the data you're looping over doesn't have a suitable unique value to use as a key, you can access the array index:

```
<tr v-for="(employee, index) in employees" :key="index">..</tr>
```

When iterating over objects, this syntax will give you the item's property name.

## v-if

Another common piece of UI logic is rendering elements conditionally. Using the `v-if` directive will cause Vue to render the element only if the data property or expression evaluates as truthy:

```
<tbody>
  <tr v-for="employee in employees">
    ...
  </tr>
  <tr v-if="employees.length === 0">
    <td colspan="6">No employees found</td>
  </tr>
</tbody>
```

The code above will display a fallback message if the `employees` array is empty. This is useful for code where the data is being loaded dynamically (that is, from an API).

As you might expect, there's also a `v-else` counterpart, as well as `v-else-if`, to allow you to handle more complex conditions:

```
<tbody>
```

```
  <tr v-for="employee in employees"> ... </tr>
  <tr v-if="isLoadingData">
    <td colspan="6"><img src="spinner.gif" /></td>
  </tr>
  <tr v-else-if="employees.length === 0">
    <td colspan="6">No employees found</td>
  </tr>
</tbody>
```

Here, `v-if` and `v-else-if` are used in conjunction to display a loading spinner if the `isLoading` property is true, or a fallback message if `isLoading` is false and there are no employees.

## v-bind

Often you'll want to take data from your instance and pass it as an attribute to an HTML element—for example, using a URL string as an `href` or `src` attribute.

Going back to our example, we'll bind each employee's profile photo to the `img` element using the `v-bind` directive:

```
  <img v-bind:src="employee.photoUrl" class="ui mini rounded image" />
```

By doing this, Vue knows to update the attribute any time the bound property changes.

Vue allows you to use a shorthand for binding attributes, prefixing them with `:` rather than the more verbose `v-bind:`.

```
  <img :src="employee.photoUrl" class="ui mini rounded image" />
```

We'll be using this shorter syntax throughout the rest of the book.

## v-model

Vue also includes two-way binding for use with form inputs. This allows changes to the input to update the data property:

```
<div id="app">
  <input v-model="text" placeholder="edit me">
  <p>Text is: {{ text }}</p>
</div>

<script>
new Vue({
  el: '#app',
  data: {
    text: 'Good golly, Miss Molly'
  }
});
</script>
```

 **Take It for a Spin**

You can try out this example at <u>CodeSandbox</u>[2].

In the example above, the `v-model` directive is being used to bind the `text` property to the `<input>` element. When Vue initially renders the template, the input will be pre-filled with the content of `text`. Changing the input field will cause the `text` property to be updated and the output inside the `<p>` element to be re-rendered.

### v-on

We can use the `v-on:<event>` syntax for attaching listeners to events that are emitted by elements and components:

```
<button v-on:click="heading = 'Hello World!'">Click Me</button>
```

In the example above, the `heading` property on our instance data would be set to "Hello, World!" when the button is clicked. As with interpolations, the values you

---

pass to directives can include any valid JavaScript expression, and can directly reference instance data properties as if they were local variables.

Vue allows you to use a shorthand for binding event handlers, prefixing them with `@` rather than the more verbose `v-on:`. We'll be using this shorter syntax throughout the rest of the book.

As well as modifying data properties, you can also call custom methods on your Vue instance. The method will receive the event object as the first argument.

**JavaScript**

```javascript
new Vue({
  el: "#main",
  data: {
    status: ""
  },
  methods: {
    updateStatus(event) {
      const buttons = ['left', 'middle', 'right'];
      this.status = `You clicked the ${buttons[event.button]} button.`;
    }
  }
});
```

**Template**

```html
<div id="main">
  <button @mousedown="updateStatus" @contextmenu.prevent="">Toggle Me!</button>
  <p>{{ status }}</p>
</div>
```

 **Check Out a Demo**

You can see a working example of this at [CodeSandbox](#)[3].

In the example above, we attach a handler to the button's *mousedown* event.

Within the handler, we inspect the event object to find out which mouse button was clicked and display it to the user.

There's a second handler listening in to the  *contextmenu*  event, as we want to prevent the browser's context menu from appearing when right-clicking. We don't actually need a handler function here, as Vue has some built-in modifiers we can chain on to events for common use cases.

Some of the most common ones are:

- **.stop**. This stops propagation of the event (like calling `event.stopPropagation()` ).
- **.prevent**. This prevents the default action from being fired (like calling `event.preventDefault()` ).
- **.capture**. Use event capturing when listening.
- **.once**. This attaches the handler to listen for the first firing of the event only.

There are quite a few others available, so I recommend checking them out in the Vue documentation[4].

# Methods

Defining your own methods helps keep your UI logic together and out of your template. This helps keep the templates clean and readable and makes your logic easier to test.

As we briefly saw in the previous section, you can define custom methods on your Vue instance by adding them to an object under the  *methods*  property:

```
methods: {
  updateStatus(event) {
    const buttons = ['left', 'middle', 'right'];
    this.status = `You clicked the ${buttons[event.button]} button.`;
```

---

3. https://codesandbox.io/s/nn43m8p4nj
4. https://vuejs.org/v2/guide/events.html#Event-Modifiers

```
    }
  }
```

Vue binds these methods to the instance so that other methods and data are available as properties of `this`, meaning we can easily access all of our instance data and call other methods.

As with data properties, methods are available directly in the template scope.

 **Template Scope**

> Vue templates have access to all the data and methods defined on the instance they're rendered from. They *don't* have access to built-in browser APIs (such as `console.log`), so you'll need to wrap these in an instance method in order to call them from the template.

## Computed Properties

There are often times when you'll want to use a custom method to compute some derived data to use in your template. The problem is that you want to avoid computationally expensive methods being called more often than necessary. Vue's solution to this is "computed properties".

A **computed property** is actually a function whose output is cached and returned on subsequent calls (similar to a memoized function). If the function depends on an item of reactive data, and that data changes, the function will be re-run and the output re-cached.

However, if something else changes in the Vue instance (such as another property that's independent of the computed property being updated), the cached result will be returned and we'll be spared running the (potentially expensive) function.

To see this in practice, along with some of the other concepts presented in this chapter, let's add some basic functionality to our staff directory.

It would be nice to sort the table according to which column header is clicked by the user. Let's start by adding a *sortBy* property to our instance data, and give it a default value:

```
data: {
  heading: "Staff Directory",
  sortBy: "firstName"
  employees: [
    ...
  ]
}
```

Next, we'll need to add event handlers to our column headers to change the *sortBy* value when clicked:

```
<tr>
  <th>Avatar</th>
  <th @click="sortBy = 'firstName'">First Name</th>
  <th @click="sortBy = 'lastName'">Last Name</th>
  <th @click="sortBy = 'email'">Email</th>
  <th @click="sortBy = 'phone'">Phone</th>
  <th @click="sortBy = 'department'">Department</th>
</tr>
```

Finally, let's create a computed property that returns an array of employees sorted according to our *sortBy* property:

```
computed: {
  sortedEmployees() {
    return this.employees.sort((a, b) => a[this.sortBy].localeCompare(b[this.
    ↪sortBy]))
  }
}
```

All we need to do now is swap out the reference to *employees* in our template's *v-for* loop for our new *sortedEmployees* computed property!

```
<tr v-for="(employee, index) in sortedEmployees" :key="index">
```

```
    . . .
  </tr>
```

Note that we reference computed properties as if they were normal reactive data properties, rather than functions.

Thanks to Vue's internal magic, the output value of `sortedEmployees` is cached and will only be recomputed if the `sortBy` property changes, or if the `employees` array is modified.

## Staff Directory

| Avatar | First Name | Last Name | Email | Phone | Department |
|--------|-----------|-----------|-------|-------|------------|
|  | amelia | austin | amelia.austin@example.com | (651)-507-3705 | Engineering |
| | tammy | gibson | tammy.gibson@example.com | (815)-727-0663 | Support |
| | brandon | griffin | brandon.griffin@example.com | (509)-317-9506 | Management |
| | bobbie | murphy | bobbie.murphy@example.com | (925)-667-7604 | Management |
| | kristin | terry | kristin.terry@example.com | (021)-544-1184 | Sales |

1-3. Sorting staff by last name

### Live Demos

Check out the live demo of our code so far at CodeSandbox[5].

As an added bonus, here's another version that includes an input field to filter the staff by last name[6].

---

[5.] https://codesandbox.io/s/mo27p57pvy
[6.] https://codesandbox.io/s/ypom8z2j0z

## Summary

Now that we've come to the end of the first chapter, you should have a clear idea of why Vue is a good choice for projects of all sizes and complexity.

We looked through what makes up a simple Vue application, seeing how we can give Vue data to observe and render to the screen, and using directives to create templates that are dynamically updated as the data changes.

We also looked at how to create methods that can be called from within a Vue template, and how computed properties can be used to efficiently compute items of derived state.

Lastly, we took the basic HTML staff directory table and rebuilt it in Vue, to get comfortable with using some of its features and giving us a nice example we can build on in later chapters.

# Vue Tooling

Chapter

2

Like the other established frameworks out there, a collection of tooling has sprung up around Vue. By tooling, I'm referring to software whose job is to facilitate the development of applications (such as code generation), prepare it for release or deployment (for example, compilation and packaging), or facilitate debugging when the inevitable bugs creep in.

In this chapter, I'd like to focus on the latter two of these categories—build tooling, and debugging. Both are well served by official Vue tools, which we'll be taking a look at.

# Why Use Build Tooling?

While including Vue from a CDN can be a good option when you're just starting out, or when you're whipping up a quick proof-of-concept app, we'll want to introduce some build tools to assist us in producing modern, modular, and efficient JavaScript that's ready for production.

Having a good build tooling setup will pay dividends by automating much of the work of preparing your code for deployment. Not only that, but it ensures the process is reliable and repeatable and removes the opportunity for human error (for example, forgetting to perform a step in a manual process).

Let's take a brief look at some of the most common tasks handled by modern build tooling.

## Transpilation: Using Modern JavaScript Syntax in Old Browsers

The newer syntax and features (> ES2015) facilitate more concise, readable code, as well as making JavaScript a more pleasant language to develop in. Even though all modern browsers now support ES2015 (aka ES6), you don't always have the luxury of ignoring older browsers.

By adding a build step with Babel[1], you can transpile your code back to an older

---

[1.] https://babeljs.io/

version (including some polyfills where necessary) and support older browsers without having to give up the modern language features.

As a bonus, by introducing transpilation we can also adopt more cutting-edge features before they've gained widespread browser support!

## Linting: Ensuring Code Quality

A must-have tool for serious JavaScript developers these days is the code linter. A linter can be run during development and/or during a build step, scanning your code for syntax errors as you type. Many popular code editors and IDEs can be configured to display these errors as you type, giving you real-time feedback and helping to prevent bugs from creeping into your code.

ESLint[2], one of the most popular linters, can also be configured to check if your code conforms to pre-defined sets of rules for coding conventions and even code style preferences. There's even an official Vue plugin for ESLint (eslint-plugin-vue, discussed below), which will help you produce idiomatic code that adheres to recommended best practices.

## Using Single-file Components

One major benefit of introducing a build step is that you can also start using Vue's single-file components (SFCs) within your application. SFCs allow you to combine the template, code, and styling for a component within a single file with a *.vue* extension.

The advantages of keeping the logic and UI for a component together in the same file are twofold: the components are easier to maintain, as all the necessary parts are kept together and not spread out through the file system; and because each component is self-contained, the code is much easier to reuse in other projects.

**ExampleComponent.vue**

---

[2.] https://eslint.org/

```
<template>
  <div class="example">{{ msg }}</div>
</template>

<script>
export default {
  data () {
    return {
      msg: 'Hello world!'
    }
  }
}
</script>

<style>
.example {
  color: red;
}
</style>
```

Using the vue-loader webpack plugin, the HTML inside the `<template>` tags is compiled to JavaScript code that's minified and bundled into your application, along with the component JavaScript from within the `<script>` tags.

`<style>` tags can be used to include style rules in CSS, or a number of other formats (specified by a `lang` attribute). These are extracted by the plugin and piped through other CSS rules you've set up in your webpack configuration. By adding the `scoped` attribute to the tag, the resulting styles will be identified by a unique hash, preventing them from affecting any other components in the app.

## Minification: Saving Space (and User Bandwidth)

While including libraries and script files via individual `<script>` tags is fine for simpler use cases, for production code you'll want to be optimizing your application to make the best use of your users' bandwidth and provide an optimal experience.

In the case of Vue, building the code for production provides a performance benefit: your templates are compiled down to JavaScript, meaning that your application no longer needs to include the template compiler as part of the bundled code.

# Vue CLI

The average client-side JavaScript project will utilize a range of build tools including transpilers, linters, minifiers and module bundlers, and each of these tools has its own configuration options that often need to be set a certain way in order to play nicely with the other tools in the chain.

A number of boilerplate projects have sprung up to take the pain out of setting up new apps, by providing a pre-configured starting point that you can build on, rather than start from scratch. These can work out well if you're able find a boilerplate project that includes the set of tools you want to use.

Vue's CLI (command-line interface) is a terminal-based tool that aims to solve this problem in a different way, allowing you to create new projects by selecting preset combinations, or picking and choosing the build tools you want and having the CLI install and configure them for you.

## Installing the CLI

Installing the CLI tool is very straightforward, and you probably won't be surprised to learn that it's done via npm. We'll be using version 3, which was recently released at the time of writing. It's installed with the following command:

```
npm install -g @vue/cli
```

The above will install Vue CLI as a global module, meaning you can access it from any directory on your system directly from your terminal/command prompt.

 **Prerequisites**

You'll need Node/npm and Git installed to be able to use Vue CLI. I recommend using **nvm** to <u>install and manage Node.js on your system</u>[3].

## Setting up New Projects

To start a new Vue project from the terminal you use the *vue create* command, followed by the name of the project:

```
vue create my-new-project
```

This command will create a folder in the current directory with the name of the project you provided. After pressing enter, an interactive prompt will launch and allow you to choose between starting from a preset or manually selecting features.

2-1. A prompt for choosing features

On a fresh install of the CLI, the only preset available is *default (babel, eslint)* , which will set up your project with transpilation and code linting, which

---

3. https://www.sitepoint.com/quick-tip-multiple-versions-node-nvm/

includes the "essential" Vue ruleset.

If you choose a preset, Vue CLI will then set up your project folder as a local Git repository, create a skeleton application structure, and run *npm install* under the hood to pull in any dependencies.

 **Automatic Project Source Control**

The CLI will not only initialize your project folder as a Git repo but will make the first commit for you. This means that you're free to start experimenting right away, and can easily revert to your original state by running *git reset --hard* .

Once it's finished, you should be left with something like this:

```
├── babel.config.js
├── node_modules (omitted for brevity)
├── package.json
├── package-lock.json
├── public
│   ├── favicon.ico
│   └── index.html
├── README.md
└── src
    ├── App.vue
    ├── assets
    │   └── logo.png
    ├── components
    │   └── HelloWorld.vue
    └── main.js
```

After changing into the new project directory, there are several npm scripts pre-configured that you can use:

- *npm run serve* . This will start a local development server and compile the project files. The process will watch the files in your *src* folder and recompile on any changes.

▨    `npm run build` . This command will compile your project, creating an optimized production build.

▨    `npm run lint` . This will run the linter on your source files, checking them for compliance with the rulesets specified in the `eslintConfig` section of the project's `package.json` file.

The generated `package.json` file is also worth a quick look:

```json
{
  "name": "my-new-project",
  "version": "0.1.0",
  "private": true,
  "scripts": {
    "serve": "vue-cli-service serve",
    "build": "vue-cli-service build",
    "lint": "vue-cli-service lint"
  },
  "dependencies": {
    "vue": "^2.5.17"
  },
  "devDependencies": {
    "@vue/cli-plugin-babel": "^3.0.1",
    "@vue/cli-plugin-eslint": "^3.0.1",
    "@vue/cli-service": "^3.0.1",
    "vue-template-compiler": "^2.5.17"
  },
  "eslintConfig": {
    "root": true,
    "env": {
      "node": true
    },
    "extends": [
      "plugin:vue/essential",
      "eslint:recommended"
    ],
    "rules": {},
    "parserOptions": {
      "parser": "babel-eslint"
    }
  },
  "postcss": {
```

```
    "plugins": {
      "autoprefixer": {}
    }
  },
  "browserslist": [
    "> 1%",
    "last 2 versions",
    "not ie <= 8"
  ]
}
```

As you can see, ESLint has been set up with the *recommended* ruleset, and the `vue/essential` plugin (which you can read more about in the **ESLint plugin's** **repo**[4]. Babel has also been configured to support all the browsers covered by the `broswerslist` options.

While the default preset is a good starting point for learning about build tooling in Vue apps, and for building quick prototypes, for proper applications you're probably going to want to customize the project by selecting the features you want.

 **Webpack Configuration**

> Vue CLI is built on top of webpack but abstracts away all the configuration to make it easier to get up and running. You can see the webpack configuration at any time by running the `vue inspect` command.

Running Vue CLI and choosing to manually select features presents you with the following screen:

---

[4.] https://github.com/vuejs/eslint-plugin-vue

```
Terminal - njacques@Vostro-3500 ~/Code        —  +  ×

File  Edit  View  Terminal  Tabs  Help
Vue CLI v3.0.1
? Please pick a preset: Manually select features
? Check the features needed for your project: (Press <space> to
  select, <a> to toggle all, <i> to invert selection)
)● Babel
 ○ TypeScript
 ○ Progressive Web App (PWA) Support
 ○ Router
 ○ Vuex
 ○ CSS Pre-processors
 ● Linter / Formatter
 ○ Unit Testing
 ○ E2E Testing
```

2-2. A screen offering manual selection of features

## Plugins

Let's take a look at the available plugins.

- **Babel**. As in the "default" preset, this will set up your project to transpile ES2015+ code back to JavaScript ES5 for wider browser compatibility.
- **TypeScript**. This sets up the TypeScript compiler, so you can write your code with the benefit of static typing.
- **Progressive Web App (PWA) Support**. This plugin will add all of the boilerplate files necessary to create an installable PWA with custom icons and offline support. We'll take a closer look at PWAs later in the book.
- **Router**. If you need client-side routing, this option will pre-install the official Vue Router library. We'll be looking into routing in Vue apps in Chapter 4.
- **Vuex**. This option will set up your project with Vuex, which is the official state management solution for more complex Vue apps. We'll dive deeper into Vuex in Chapter 5.

- **CSS Pre-processors**. Selecting this option will lead to a further screen allowing you to choose from SCSS/Sass, LESS, and Stylus plugins. Note that by default, Vue CLI supports PostCSS, Autoprefixer and CSS Modules.
- **Linter / Formatter**. This option will give you the choice of installing ESLint by itself, or in combination with the Airbnb config, Standard config, or the Prettier code formatter.
- **Unit Testing**. Selecting unit testing will give you the option to install Mocha and Chai, or Jest as your testing tools.
- **E2E Testing**. Similarly to the unit testing option, choosing E2E testing will let you choose between installing Cypress and Nightwatch.

After you've made your selections, the CLI will ask you how you want to store your configuration options (in separate files, or in `package.json`) and then allow you to save your current plugin selection as a preset for future use.

You can also add plugins to existing projects that were generated with the CLI tool. This is a big plus point for Vue CLI, as you're not locked into the choices you make when starting a project and, unlike **create-react-app** (for example), you don't have to "eject" from the tool in order to customize your project's configuration.

From within the project directory, simply run the `vue add` command with the name of the plugin:

```
vue add @vue/cli-plugin-typescript
# or
vue add @vue/typescript
```

The two commands above are equivalent and will both install the TypeScript plugin. Vue CLI automatically expands the shorthand version for you.

It's also possible to install third-party CLI plugins by omitting the `@vue` prefix. The following command will install the unofficial Apollo plugin:

```
vue add apollo
```

The official Vue CLI plugins are listed in the documentation at **cli.vuejs.org**[5], but there's currently no list of third-party plugins.

## Browser Devtools

As I mentioned at the start of the chapter, Vue also has tooling to aid with debugging, in the form of the Vue devtools. The devtools are available as a browser plugin for both Chrome and Firefox, and as a cross-platform Electron app, which can also debug Vue apps running on mobile devices.

If you've developed applications with React before, the Vue devtools combine functionality similar to that of the React and Redux extensions.

The tools allow you to take a look into a running Vue application, providing three different tabs to help you inspect and debug your code.

I recommend installing one of the browser extensions (you can find the links on **GitHub**[6]) and trying the devtools with the examples from this book.

---

[5] https://cli.vuejs.org/

[6] https://github.com/vuejs/vue-devtools#installation

## Components Tab

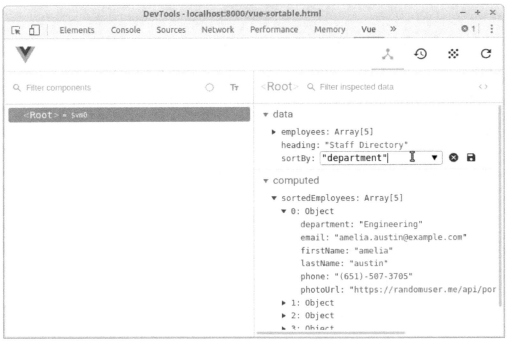

2-3. An example of the Vue devtools components tab

The first section gives you a hierarchical view of all the components that make up your application. Selecting a component from the tree allows you to inspect its state (that is, its `data` object) in the right-hand pane, where the values can be dynamically edited while the app runs.

When a component is selected, it's also then available to interact with programmatically from the browser's console, assigned to the variable `$vm0`. You can read and write to data values, and call any of the component's methods.

We'll revisit this tab in our next chapter on components.

## Vuex Tab

2-4. An example of the Vuex tab

This tab is only active if a Vuex store is detected in the application. It allows you to examine the state of the store at any point in time, and all the mutations that have been committed. You can even move back and forth through the mutations, effectively time-traveling through the state of your application.

If this isn't making much sense to you right now, don't worry; we'll be covering Vuex in a later chapter.

## Events Tab

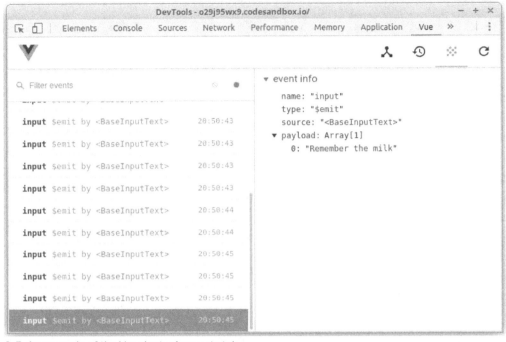

2-5. An example of the Vue devtools events tab

The events tab aggregates all the events emitted by your application, from anywhere in the component tree. Selecting an event will display more information about it in the right-hand pane, allowing you to see which component emitted it and any payload that was sent.

# Editor/IDE Integrations

Due to its popularity, there are also Vue plugins and extensions available for many of the popular code editors and IDEs. These can offer anything from syntax highlighting for `.vue` files to autocompletion and code generation.

One of the most fully featured plugins currently available is the <u>Vetur extension</u>[7] for Visual Studio Code (VS Code). As well as syntax highlighting and

---

[7] https://github.com/vuejs/vetur

autocompletion, it provides snippets for scaffolding common tasks (such as new components), code formatting support, debugging, and autocomplete support for popular libraries such as Vue Router, and <u>Vuetify</u>[8].

### Installing Vetur for VS Code

1.  Fire up VS Code and go to the Extensions menu on the left sidebar.

2.  Into the search bar, type "vetur".

3.  Select the Vetur extension (by Pine Wu) from the results, and hit the **install**

button.

## Summary

In this chapter, we looked at the benefits of introducing a build step to your Vue applications, and how you can easily install and configure the necessary build tools for new projects using the Vue CLI.

We also looked briefly at the Vue devtools, which are a must-have resource when working with Vue applications. If you haven't already done so, I recommend installing them now, as we'll be using them in the next chapter as we take a look at components.

---

[8.] https://vuetifyjs.com/en/

# Components

Chapter

3

As we briefly touched on in <u>Chapter 1</u>, Vue was designed for creating component-based UIs. The idea is that you can structure your application around self-contained, reusable elements that represent a discrete part of the interface.

One example of this might be an Avatar component that displays a user's profile picture as a circular image. Once created, this component can be dropped into your application code anywhere you want to display the user's avatar:

```
<div class="sidebar">
  <avatar :src="user.image" />
  <h2>{{ user.nick }}</h2>
</div>
```

As you can see in the above example, using a Vue component in your templates is like having a new HTML element available: you use the component's name as the tag ( `<avatar>` , in this case) and pass in any data it needs in the form of custom attributes. (Here a URL is being passed as the `src` attribute. We'll look at this in more detail soon.)

## Defining Custom Components

So how do we go about creating our own components with Vue?

The Vue object (which is a global, if you include it from a CDN) provides a `component` method. This can be used to register new components by passing a name and an options object, similar to the one we used to create our Vue instance in Chapter 1:

```
Vue.component('MyCustomComponent', {
  // ...
});
```

**A Note on Naming**

You can choose kebab case (my-custom-component) or Pascal case (MyCustomComponent) when naming your component. I recommend Pascal case, as this will allow you to use either when referencing your component within a template. It's important to note that when using your component directly in the DOM (as in <u>Chapter 1</u>), *only* the kebab case tag name is valid.

Registering a component in this way makes it available anywhere in your Vue app for other components to use within their templates. This is very handy for components (for example, general layout components) that you're going to be using a lot throughout your app.

When using **single file components** (SFCs), it's possible to import and use these directly within the components where they're needed, which we'll cover in the next section.

## Component Options

Components take almost all the same options you can use when creating an instance, with a couple of important differences.

Firstly, components don't accept an `el` property: you can supply a component with a template by setting the `template` property to a string containing markup.

### Template String

```
Vue.component('HelloWorld', {
  template: '<p>Hello, world!</p>',
});
```

If the string starts with a `#`, Vue will treat it as a selector and look for a matching element in the DOM. If it finds one, it will use its contents as the template.

**In-DOM Template**

```
Vue.component('HelloWorld', {
  template: '#my-template-container-id'
});
```

If you're using SFCs, you can provide your markup within `<template></template>` tags in your `.vue` component file.

**HelloWorld.vue**

```
<template>
  <p>Hello, world!</p>
</template>

<script>
  export default {
    name: 'HelloWorld'
  }
</script>
```

The second change is that a component's `data` property must be a function that returns a new object literal. Think of this function like a factory, providing a fresh data object to each instance of the component that's created:

```
Vue.component('HelloWorld', {
  template: 'Hello, {{message}}!',
  data() {
    return {
      message: 'World'
    }
  }
});
```

Let's revisit our staff directory example from Chapter 1 and convert it into a component. This way, we can easily reuse it on different screens of a web app.

## Online Example

Note that I'm using the expanded example from the <u>online example</u>[1].

We'll implement it as a `.vue` SFC, so if you haven't already, install the Vue CLI as described in <u>Chapter 2</u> and create a new project using the default preset.

Open the project folder, navigate into `src/components`, and create a file called `StaffDirectory.vue`. Inside this file, add the following code.

**src/components/StaffDirectory.vue (template)**

```
<template>
  <div class="ui container">
    <input v-model="filterBy" placeholder="Filter By Last Name">
    <table class="ui celled table">
      <thead>
        <tr>
          <th>Avatar</th>
          <th @click="sortBy = 'firstName'">First Name</th>
          <th @click="sortBy = 'lastName'">Last Name</th>
          <th @click="sortBy = 'email'">Email</th>
          <th @click="sortBy = 'phone'">Phone</th>
          <th @click="sortBy = 'department'">Department</th>
        </tr>
      </thead>
      <tbody>
        <tr v-for="(employee, index) in sortedEmployees" :key="index">
          <td>
            <img :src="employee.photoUrl" class="ui mini rounded image" />
          </td>
          <td>{{ employee.firstName }}</td>
          <td>{{ employee.lastName }}</td>
          <td>{{ employee.email }}</td>
          <td>{{ employee.phone }}</td>
          <td>{{ employee.department }}</td>
        </tr>
      </tbody>
```

---

[1]. https://codesandbox.io/s/ypom8z2j0z

```
      <tfoot>
        <tr>
          <th colspan="6">{{sortedEmployees.length}} employees</th>
        </tr>
      </tfoot>
    </table>
  </div>
</template>
```

Nothing has changed in our template markup; it's just been dropped into an SFC between a pair of `<template>` tags.

One important thing to note is that (for now, at least) your templates must have a *single* root element (in this case, the `<div class="ui container"></div>` wrapper). You can't have multiple root-level elements.

**src/components/StaffDirectory.vue (script)**

```
<script>
  export default {
    name: 'StaffDirectory',
    data() {
      return {
        filterBy: "",
        sortBy: 'department',
        employees: [
          // omitted for brevity
        ]
      }
    },
    computed: {
      sortedEmployees() {
        return this.employees.filter(
          employee => employee.lastName.includes(this.filterBy)
        ).sort(
          (a, b) => a[this.sortBy].localeCompare(b[this.sortBy])
        );
      }
    }
  }
```

```
  </script>
```

For the code, we have to add an export statement to allow it to be imported and used by the other components in our app.

You might notice that our component has a `name` property. This is important for components that aren't registered globally. (We'll look at how to import components locally in a moment.) It also helps with debugging: without it, the Vue devtools will show `<AnonymousComponent>` in the component tab, making debugging difficult.

### src/StaffDirectory.vue (style)

```
<style>
  h1.ui.center.header {
    margin-top: 3em;
  }

  .ui.table th:not(:first-child):hover {
    cursor: pointer;
  }

  input {
    padding: 3px;
  }
</style>
```

We've also got some additional CSS styles to tweak the layout and change the cursor when hovering over the column headers. These are included within the style block.

We're going to use this component from within the existing `src/App.vue` file. As we've not registered it globally with Vue (that is, by calling `Vue.component()`), we have to import our new file and register it locally.

### src/App.vue

```
<template>
  <div id="app">
    <h1 class="ui center aligned header">Staff Directory</h1>
    <StaffDirectory />
  </div>
</template>

<script>
import 'semantic-ui-css/semantic.css'
import StaffDirectory from './components/StaffDirectory.vue'

export default {
  name: 'app',
  components: {
    StaffDirectory
  }
}
</script>
```

Within the `<script>` section, we import the `StaffDirectory` component. You can replace the `HelloWorld` import here, as we aren't going to use it.

 **Importing Styles**

> In Chapter 1, I included a CSS library called Semantic UI[2] to style the staff directory. In the example above, we're importing it into our SFC instead of including it from a CDN. If you're following along, you'll need to run `npm install semantic-ui-css` from within your project directory.

The next thing we do is create a `components` property. This should be an object where each key/value pair is the component name and the component object respectively. I've used the ES2015 shorthand syntax here, as I want to use the same name we import the component with.

Lastly, we modify the template to include our new component element. We can use it in self-closing form unless we want it to wrap any child elements (we'll look

---

[2] https://semantic-ui.com/

at this later).

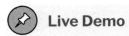

**Live Demo**

You can find this example online at <u>CodeSandbox</u>[3].

## Lifecycle Methods

If you've used React before, you're probably familiar with the concept of **component lifecycle methods**. The idea behind this is that there are various events that happen in the lifetime of a component—from when it's created, through to when it's destroyed. The lifecycle methods are called at these points, allowing you to execute code—for example, to perform an Ajax request when the component is initialized.

The Vue documentation includes a <u>useful chart of all of the various methods and when in the lifecycle they're called</u>[4].

The methods you'll probably find yourself using most often are:

- **created**. This is the place to kick off any Ajax requests for fetching data.
- **mounted**. When this hook is fired, the component has been rendered and inserted into the DOM. This is where you can manipulate the DOM elements—for example, if you're wrapping a non-Vue library of some sort.
- **beforeDestroy**. Just before the component is removed from the DOM, this method is called. You can do any cleanup here.

If we wanted to load in the staff data for our component from an API, we could do something like the following.

**src/StaffDirectory.vue**

---

[3]. https://codesandbox.io/s/6zry10r43
[4]. https://vuejs.org/images/lifecycle.png

```
<script>
  export default {
    name: 'StaffDirectory',
    data() {
      return {
        heading: "Staff Directory",
        sortBy: 'department',
        employees: []
      }
    },
    created() {
      fetch('https://randomuser.me/api/?nat=us,dk,fr,gb&results=5')
        .then(response => response.json())
        .then(json => this.employees = json.results);
    },
    computed: {
      // ...
    }
  }
</script>
```

This way, as soon as the component is created, the `created()` method will be fired, making an Ajax request to the API and assigning the results to the `employees` data property.

## Passing Data In

Of course, being able to create reusable segments of your UI is quite handy in itself, but to be really useful we need to be able to pass information to our components—both data for it to display, and options to configure how it behaves.

Vue's way of doing this is to allow your components to declare a set of **props**, which are essentially custom attributes. To declare the props that a component will accept, you can simply add a property called *props* whose value is an array containing the names of the props as strings.

In the case of our imaginary *Avatar* components, we would declare the *src* prop that's passed in the following way:

```
{
    template: '<div class="avatar"><img :src="src" /></div>'
    name: 'Avatar',
    props: ['src']
}
```

Props are automatically available in the component's template and are accessible as properties of the component (that is, `this`) within methods and computed properties.

## Prop Validation and Defaults

Declaring props as an array of strings is fine for some situations—such as when you're just experimenting and haven't settled on your component design yet. To build more robust components, though, it's essential to be able to enforce the type and content of a component's props and provide default values. These abilities are especially important for situations where other developers may be using components created by you.

To apply some basic type validation to your props, you have to set your component's *props* property to an object where the prop name is the key, and the type is the value:

```
props: {
    myString: String,
    myNumber: Number,
    myBoolean: Boolean,
    myArray: Array,
    myObject: Object
}
```

If you try to pass a value of the wrong type, you'll get a warning in the browser's console.

With our *props* object, we now have the flexibility to do more in terms of prop validation. If we want, instead of using the prop type as the value, we can set it to an object:

```
props: {
  isAdminUser: {
    type: Boolean,
    required: true
  }
}
```

As you can see, we're explicitly setting a `type` property now, along with a `required` boolean. There are two other options we can also now set: `default`, and `validate`.

The `default` property is used in the event that no value is passed to the component for that prop:

```
props: {
  isAdminUser: {
    type: Boolean,
    default: false
  }
}
```

### 📢 Defaults for Arrays and Objects

As arrays and objects in JavaScript are passed by reference, any default value *must* be a factory function that returns a new object or array each time.

In cases where you want to do some more complex validation than just checking the prop's type, you can provide a `validate()` function, which will receive the incoming prop and return a boolean value to indicate validity:

```
props: {
  user: {
    validate(user) {
      return ['admin', 'editor', 'author'].includes(user.role);
    }
```

```
      }
  }
```

In the example above, the validation function checks to ensure the `user` prop is
an object with one of the specified roles.

## Communicating with the Outside World

So far, we've seen how to get data into a component, using props, but how do we
allow our component to communicate information back? In React, it's common to
pass a callback function to a component to allow for data to be sent back.
Although it's also possible to do this in Vue, the preferred way is to use events.

We previously looked at how to listen for DOM events (such as mouse clicks) on
HTML elements in the template and connect them up to handler methods. It's
actually very straightforward to have components emit their own, custom events,
and listen for them in exactly the same way.

**SearchBox.vue**

```
<template>
  <div class="searchbox">
    <label>
      Terms
      <input v-model="terms" />
    </label>
    <button @click="$emit('search', terms)">Search</button>
  </div>
</template>

<script>
export default {
  name: 'SearchBox',
  data() {
    return {
      terms: ''
    }
  }
```

```
}
</script>
```

In the code above, we have a simple  `SearchBox`  component that renders a text
input with a label, and a button. When the button is clicked, the component emits
a  `search`  event that the parent component can listen for.

**Parent Component**

```
<template>
  ...
  <SearchBox @search="onSearch" />
  ...
</template>

<script>
import SearchBox from 'src/components/SearchBox.vue';

export default {
  components: {
    SearchBox
  },
  methods: {
    onSearch(terms) {
      // make API call with search terms
    }
  }
}
</script>
```

In our imaginary parent component, we're rendering the  `SearchBox`  component
and attaching a handler to the  `search`  event. When the event fires, the
`onSearch`  method is called, receiving the  `terms`  as a parameter, which it can
then use to make an API call.

# Slots

In all the examples so far, I've shown the components used as self-closing
elements. In order to make components that can be composed together in useful

ways, we need to be able to nest them inside one another as we do with HTML elements.

If you try to use a component with a closing tag and put some content inside, you'll see that Vue just swallows this up. Anything within the component's opening and closing tags is replaced with the rendered output from the component itself:

```
<StaffDirectory>
  <p>This content will be replaced.</p>
</StaffDirectory>
```

Vue lets us output the children of a component by providing a `<slot>` component that can be placed in the template at the location you want to render the child elements.

### TodoList.vue

```
<template>
  <div class="todo-list">
    <h2>To-do List</h2>
    <ul>
      <slot><li>All done!</li></slot>
    </ul>
  </div>
</template>

<script>
  export default {
    name: 'TodoList'
  }
</script>
```

### Parent Template

```
<TodoList>
  <li>Buy some milk</li>
  <li>Feed the cats</li>
```

```
    <li>Have some pie</li>
  </TodoList>
```

In the example above, the `TodoList` component will render any child elements inside a `<ul>` with a heading.

 **Slot Fallback Content**

> The `<slot>` element can have its own child content, which will be rendered in the event that the component itself has no children. This is useful for providing default or fallback content.

## Named Slots

Your components' slots can actually be named, meaning you can have multiple slots rendered in different locations in the template. This allows you to design very flexible components that are highly configurable.

As an example, let's say we wanted to create a reusable Bootstrap card component[5] for our application, with slots to provide header, footer, and body content.

**HeaderFooterCard.vue (template only)**

```
<template>
<div class="card text-center">
  <div class="card-header">
    <slot name="header"></slot>
  </div>
  <div class="card-body">
    <slot name="body"></slot>
  </div>
  <div class="card-footer text-muted">
    <slot name="footer"></slot>
  </div>
```

---

5. https://getbootstrap.com/docs/4.1/components/card/

```
    </div>
  </template>
```

## Usage

```
<HeaderFooterCard>
  <template slot="header">Featured</template>

  <template slot="body">
    <h5 class="card-title">Special title treatment</h5>
    <p class="card-text">With supporting text below as a natural lead-in to
    additional content.</p>
    <a href="#" class="btn btn-primary">Go somewhere</a>
  </template>

  <template slot="footer">Two days ago</template>
</HeaderFooterCard>
```

Now, you might be thinking that we could have used props to pass the header and footer text to the component, but using slots means you're free to pass in HTML elements and even other Vue components.

## Scoped Slots

Vue has one last trick up its sleeve where slots are concerned. It provides a clever little feature called scoped slots. **Scoped slots** allow child components to access data from the parent.

We could, for example, build a component that fetches data from an API and makes it available to any children.

### AjaxLoader.vue

```
<template>
  <div>
    <slot :data="data"></slot>
  </div>
</template>
```

```
<script>
  export default {
    name: 'AjaxLoader',
    props: {
      url: {
        type: String,
        required: true
      }
    },
    data() {
      return {
        data: []
      }
    },
    created() {
      fetch(this.url)
        .then(res => res.json())
        .then(json => this.data = json);
    }
  }
</script>
```

Note that the `<slot>` element is wrapped in a `<div>` here, as it can't be the
route element in a template. This is because whoever uses the AjaxLoader
component might pass multiple child elements.

## Usage

```
<AjaxLoader url="/api/staff">
  <template slot-scope="{ data }">
    <StaffDirectory :staff="data" />
  </template>
</AjaxLoader>
```

As you can see in the code above, you can use the `slot-scope` property to
access the data from the parent component and pass it into any child
components as props.

**AjaxLoader Example**

There's an example of the `AjaxLoader` component that you can check out <u>online</u>[6].

## Summary

In this chapter, we delved into components—how to create them, how to register them either globally or locally, and what additional options there are when creating them.

We also saw how to use props to get data into components, using type validation and default values to build more reliable code, and we looked at using custom events to communicate with parent components.

Lastly, we took a look at slots, and how they enable us to build more flexible components that can accept children, and even make their data available to them.

---

[6.] https://codesandbox.io/s/l4lvmqozqm

Chapter

# Routing

# 4

If you've built server-side web apps before, you'll be familiar with putting some thought into the URL structure of your application.

Using a client-side router will give your SPAs the advantages of a server-side web app—namely, the ability to use the browser's back and forward buttons to move through your app's screens, and the ability for the user to bookmark specific screens and/or states of your app.

Vue.js has the advantage of having a library that's not only extremely capable and well documented, but which is also the official routing solution for Vue, and is guaranteed to be maintained and kept in sync with the development of the core library.

## Installing Vue Router

The router can be easily added to your app via npm ( `npm install vue-router` ), or from the Vue CLI.

For the purposes of this chapter, let's install the router ourselves via npm and run through the steps needed to get a basic example up and running. As we go, I'll briefly explain each of the necessary parts, which we'll revisit in more depth later in the chapter.

If you haven't already, use the Vue CLI to create a new project based on the "default" preset. After it has finished installing, change directory into the project's root folder and run the following command:

```
npm install vue-router
```

Once the router library is installed, we need to configure it and add some routes to map URLs to components. Create a file called `router.js` inside the `src` folder and add the following.

**src/router.js**

```
import Vue from "vue";
import Router from "vue-router";
import Home from "./views/Home.vue";

Vue.use(Router);

export default new Router({
  routes: [
    {
      path: "/",
      name: "home",
      component: Home
    }
  ]
});
```

We start by importing both Vue itself and Vue Router. Because the router works as a plugin, it has to be registered with Vue, which we do by calling `vue.use()`.

Next, we create an instance of `Router` and pass in a configuration object. At a minimum, this needs to contain a `routes` key. This should be an array of object literals that define the URLs you want your app to respond to, and the components they map to. We'll look at route configuration in more detail shortly.

You're probably wondering about the `Home` component: we need to create that next.

 **Folder Structure**

When you install Vue Router via the CLI, it generates a `views` folder for you. It's a common convention for the top-level components (the ones that your app's routes map to, the "pages") to go inside this folder, separate from the components that represent more discrete parts of your UI. We'll stick with this convention for our examples.

**src/views/Home.vue**

```
<template>
  <div id="app">
    <h1 class="ui center aligned header">Staff Directory</h1>
    <StaffDirectory/>
  </div>
</template>

<script>
import StaffDirectory from "../components/StaffDirectory.vue";

export default {
  name: 'HomePage',
  components: { StaffDirectory }
}
</script>
```

This is very similar to the code from *App.vue* in our example from <u>Chapter 3</u>. It basically serves as a "page" in our application and will be rendered when the user navigates to the root URL (that is, */* ).

 **StaffDirectory File**

> Don't forget to create or copy across the *StaffDirectory.vue* file from the previous chapter into the **src/components** folder.

Our actual *App* component also needs amending.

### src/App.vue

```
<template>
  <router-view></router-view>
</template>

<script>
import 'semantic-ui-css/semantic.css'

export default {
  name: "App",
```

```
};
</script>

<style>
  body {
    padding: 2em;
  }
</style>
```

Here we've replaced the component's markup with a single tag:
`<router-view></router-view>` . This is one of the components that Vue Router
provides. We use it to specify where we want the component for each route
displayed when that route is active.

 **Semantic UI CSS**

> Don't forget to install the Semantic UI CSS module from npm:
>
> ```
> npm i semantic-ui-css
> ```

The last thing left to do is import our route configuration into our application's
entry point, and pass it to our main Vue instance when we initialize it.

**src/main.js**

```
import Vue from "vue";
import router from "./router";
import App from "./App";

Vue.config.productionTip = false;

new Vue({
  router,
  render: h => h(App)
}).$mount('#app');
```

In this file, we're importing the configured router instance we create in `router.js` and passing it into our main Vue instance as an option. In conjunction with having registered the router as a Vue plugin, this will make the router instance available to all components within our app.

You probably noticed that the way we're initializing the Vue instance here is a little bit different. This is due to the fact we're now using a module bundler in our project and an optimized build of Vue.js. Don't worry about this too much, as setting up your projects with the Vue CLI will autogenerate this file, as we'll see next.

## Installing via Vue CLI

Installing the router via the CLI has the added bonus of adding a basic routing configuration to your app (very similar to what we created above) so you can get up and running right away.

If you're starting a new project, choose the option to manually select features and ensure that "Router" is checked. See <u>Chapter 2</u> for a more detailed run-through of using the CLI.

You can add it to an existing, CLI-created project by running `vue add @vue/ router` from inside the project folder.

## Router Config Options

The router class accepts some other useful options when you initialize it.

- **base**. The `base` option allows you to specify a base URL that will be used for all routes. If your app lives at `www.example.com/my-app/`, setting the `base` option to `my-app` will automatically include this in your app's URLs.
- **mode**. This option allows you to use the router in `hash` mode, or `history` mode. (There's a third mode, `abstract`, for server-side rendering.) Hash mode appends the current route to the app's URL as a hash fragment (for example, `www.example.com/#/blog`), which is useful for supporting legacy browsers that don't support HTML5 history mode.

History mode makes use of this support (now widespread in modern browsers) to provide URLs that are indistinguishable from server-side ones. The only caveat is that your app's back end must be configured to support it by serving your app's entry file ( *index.html* ) for every route in your application.

**Example Server Configurations**

The View Router docs have some handy <u>server configuration examples</u>[1].

**Additional Options**

The options above are the ones you'll most commonly want to configure. There are lots of additional options <u>detailed in the API documentation</u>[2].

## Routes

### Creating Routes

As we saw in the basic example at the beginning of the chapter, we define our routes by passing an array of route configuration objects to the router when we instantiate it.

As a minimum, we need to supply a path (that is, a URL) and a component for each route we want to define:

```
import HelloWorld from './components/HelloWorld';

const routes = [
```

---

[1.] https://router.vuejs.org/guide/essentials/history-mode.html#example-server-configurations

[2.] https://router.vuejs.org/api/#router-construction-options

```
  {
    path: '/hello-world',
    component: HelloWorld
  }
];
```

The above route will display the `HelloWorld` component when the user navigates to the `/hello-world` URL.

There are other useful options you might want to set when creating routes.

- **name**. You can supply a name for your route. This is optional, but I'd recommend it for all but the simplest of apps. Using named routes allows your URL structure to change without breaking your app, and can make it easier to navigate to programmatically when dealing with dynamic routes.
- **redirect**. By entering the path of another route here, you can create redirects within your app.
- **beforeEnter**. You can provide a function that will be called before the route change, allowing you to perform additional logic before continuing or canceling the navigation. Later on, we'll look at how this can be used to make certain routes available to authenticated users only.
- **meta**. You can use this option to provide an object of custom properties to be made available to the route.

 **Additional Options**

> As with the router options, there are more options you can set on routes that I haven't gone into here. I'd recommend browsing the API documentation[3] if you want to know more.

## Route Parameters

Commonly, we'll want to create routes that have dynamic segments, representing things such as a resource ID, or a blog post slug. Vue Router allows

---

3. https://router.vuejs.org/api/#routes

us to specify these dynamic segments using a parameter name prefixed with a colon.

In the case of a route for posts on a blog, we might have a route configuration something like this:

```
{
    name: 'blog',
    path: '/blog/:slug',
    component: BlogPost
}
```

Here we've given the route a name (we'll see why in the next section) and specified that the segment that comes after  */blog/*  should be assigned to the parameter  *slug* .

Within the app's components, the values of any route parameters are available as  *this.$route.params* . This could then be used to request the relevant post via Ajax.

**BlogPost.vue**

```
export default {
  name: 'BlogPost',
  data: () => ({
    title: '',
    content: ''
  }),
  created() {
    const { slug } = this.$route.params;
    fetch(`/api/posts/${slug}`)
      .then(res => res.json())
      .then(post => {
        this.title = post.title;
        this.content = post.content;
      });
  }
}
```

It's a good idea to limit your use of the `this.$route` object to your page components and pass down any parameters via props to child components that need them. This avoids coupling your UI components to the router, making them more easily reusable.

# Navigation

Changing the current route is achieved in a couple of ways: via the `<router-link>` component, and programmatically.

## Links

While you could just use a standard `<a>` tag, the `<router-link>` component that Vue Router provides has several advantages:

1. It automatically applies a CSS class of "active" when the URL matches the current route (the class name can be configured by setting the router's `linkActiveClass` option).

2. It takes into account whether the router is configured for hash mode or HTML5 history mode and will render the correct URL format automatically.

3. When in history mode, it prevents the browser from reloading the page by preventing the default click action.

4. It takes into account the `base` setting, if configured, and builds the URL accordingly.

The component is used in the same way you might use an `<a>` tag, only the URL is passed in via the `to` prop:

```
<router-link to="/hello-world">Hello, World</router-link>
```

In addition to a URL string, you can also pass in an object:

```
<router-link :to="{ path: '/hello-world' }">Hello, World</router-link>
```

The two examples above are functionally equivalent. Using an object becomes more useful when we want to set route or query parameters.

### Route parameters

```
<router-link :to="{ name: 'post', params: { postId: 2 } }">
    Hello, World
</router-link>
<!-- URL: /post/2 -->
```

### Query parameters

```
<router-link :to="{ name: 'posts', query: { sortby: date } }">
    Hello, World
</router-link>
<!-- URL: /posts?sortby=date -->
```

## Programmatic Navigation

If you need to navigate around from within the code, Vue Router provides some methods for you to interact with the browser history. Each of these methods is exposed on the router instance available inside your components as `this.$router`.

### push

The `push()` method takes a location object (in the same format that the `<router-link>` component accepts) and navigates to it. This method preserves the browser history, allowing you to return to the previous URL with the back button.

```
this.$router.push({ name: 'post', params: { postId: 2 } });
```

## replace

The `replace()` method is almost the same as `push()`, except that it replaces the current entry in the browser's history.

```
this.$router.replace({ name: 'post', params: { postId: 2 } });
```

## go

The `go()` method allows you to move around through the browser's history by supplying the number of steps to move as a positive or negative integer (to move forward or back, respectively).

```
// Return to the previous URL
this.$router.go(-1);
```

# Navigation Guards

Navigation guards provide a way to run code at certain points in the routing process. It's possible to supply callbacks that will run globally (that is, for all routes), or on a per-route basis.

Navigation guards are most commonly used to apply authorization checking to routes so part (or all) of your app can be restricted to authenticated users.

## Global Guards

Global guards can be assigned by calling any of the methods below and passing in a function that you want to be called. Multiple functions can be assigned to each guard, and will be called in the order they're registered in. Control will pass from one function to the next unless the navigation is canceled.

## beforeEach

The *beforeEach* hook is called as soon as navigation is triggered to any registered route. Callbacks are passed three arguments: *to* , *from* , and *next* .

```
router.beforeEach((to, from, next) => {
  // ...
});
```

Both *to* and *from* are route objects that contain information about the route being navigated to and the current route, respectively. From these objects, it's possible to inspect the *path* , *params* , *query* , and *hash* properties of the route.

The *next* argument is actually a callback function that your route guard must call in order to let the router know what to do next. Calling *next()* with no argument will execute the next route guard in the sequence (if any) or proceed with the navigation.

Navigation can be canceled by passing *false* , or redirected to a different route by passing a path string or location object.

## beforeResolve

This hook will fire only after any *beforeEach()* callbacks and any of the in-component guards have run (we'll come to these shortly). This is basically your last chance to abort the route change after all other guards have run (and passed), and the component itself has been loaded.

```
router.beforeResolve((to, from, next) => {
  // ...
});
```

Callback functions receive the same arguments as those registered to the *beforeEach()* guard, meaning all the same checks and outcomes are possible.

## afterEach

As the name suggests, the *afterEach()* callbacks are run after the navigation is confirmed. Callbacks receive *to* and *from* route objects, but no *next()* function, as the navigation can no longer be canceled at this stage.

```
router.afterEach((to, from) => {
  // ...
});
```

The *afterEach* hook could be used to send data about page changes to your analytics service, for example.

## Per-route guards

The per-route (and in-component) guards are useful for selectively applying logic to specific routes, but you can't assign multiple callbacks to a hook like you can with the global guards.

### beforeEnter

A *beforeEnter* guard can be set by assigning a function to a property of that name when adding a route.

```
{
  path: '/settings',
  component: SettingsPage,
  beforeEnter: (to, from, next) => {
    // ...
  }
}
```

The remainder of the guards we'll cover are assigned within page components (that is, components that are loaded directly by a route) as if they were lifecycle methods.

## beforeRouteEnter

This guard will be called when the route has been confirmed (that is, after any global  *beforeEach*  or per-route  *beforeEnter*  guards have run), but before the component itself has been created.

For this reason, you don't have access to the component via the  *this*  variable. If you need to do something with the component, such as set data, you have to pass a callback to the  *next()*  function. The callback will receive the component as an argument.

```
export default {
   name: '...',
   props: [],
   beforeRouteEnter(to, from, next) {
      // If we need access to the component
      next(component => {
         // ...
      })
   }
}
```

## beforeRouteUpdate

The  *beforeRouteUpdate*  guard will be called whenever the route changes but the component doesn't. This means that if you have a route with dynamic segments, the component will be re-used and this guard will be called, allowing you to update the display.

```
export default {
   name: '...',
   props: [],
   beforeRouteUpdate(to, from, next) {
      // ...
   }
}
```

### beforeRouteLeave

This method will be called on a component just before a route change that will navigate away from it. This gives you the opportunity to do any cleanup you may need.

```
export default {
  name: '...',
  props: [],
  beforeRouteLeave(to, from, next) {
    // ...
  }
}
```

 **Example App**

I've created a basic example app that you can navigate around[4] which logs out the various guard functions as they're activated.

Note that it's easier to see what's being logged via the CodeSandbox console, rather than your browser's console.

## Example: Authorized Routes

To put some of this into practice, let's look at something a lot of client-side apps typically need: protected routes. We'll build out a simple example that will demonstrate how to configure routes with authentication checks that will redirect to a login form when a guest tries to access them.

If you want to follow along, you should start by creating a new project with the Vue CLI, not forgetting to select the option to include Vue Router.

To keep the example simple, and focus on the routing aspects, we're going to create a mock authentication service. In a real app, this would call out to your

---

[4]. https://codesandbox.io/s/kx7xp9pvw5

server, or a third-party authentication service.

**src/auth.js**

```js
let loggedIn = false;

export default {
  login(email, password) {
    return new Promise((resolve, reject) => {
      if (email === 'user@example.com' && password === 'password') {
        loggedIn = true;
        resolve();
      } else {
        reject();
      }
    });
  },
  logout() {
    loggedIn = false;
  },
  isAuthenticated() {
    return loggedIn;
  },
};
```

This authentication service provides a `login()` method that simply checks an email and password combination, returning a promise that's resolved if the credentials match and rejected if they don't.

The login method also sets the `loggedIn` variable to `true` upon successful login, which can be checked by calling the `isAuthenticated()` method.

Next, let's create a login component to prompt users for their credentials.

**src/views/Login.vue**

```html
<template>
  <div class="ui middle aligned center aligned grid">
    <div class="column">
```

```
    <h2 class="ui teal image header">
      <div class="content">
        Log in to your account
      </div>
    </h2>
    <form class="ui large form" @submit.prevent="onSubmit" :class="{ error }">
      <div class="ui stacked segment">
        <div class="field">
          <div class="ui left icon input">
            <i class="user icon"></i>
            <input type="text" v-model="email" placeholder="E-mail address">
          </div>
        </div>
        <div class="field">
          <div class="ui left icon input">
            <i class="lock icon"></i>
            <input type="password" v-model="password" placeholder="Password">
          </div>
        </div>
        <button type="submit" class="ui fluid large teal submit button">Login
        </button>
      </div>

      <div class="ui error message">Oops, we couldn't log you in!</div>

    </form>

  </div>
  </div>
</template>

<script>
import authAPI from '../auth';

export default {
  name: 'Login',
  data: () => ({
    email: null,
    password: null,
    error: false,
  }),
  methods: {
    onSubmit() {
```

```
    authAPI.login(this.email, this.password)
      .then(() => this.$router.push('/users/1'))
      .catch(() => { this.error = true; });
    },
  },
};
</script>
```

The login form, taken from the Semantic UI examples at <u>semantic-ui.com</u>[5], is pretty straightforward. There's a method called *onSubmit()* that's attached to the form's *submit* event, which calls the auth service with the input values.

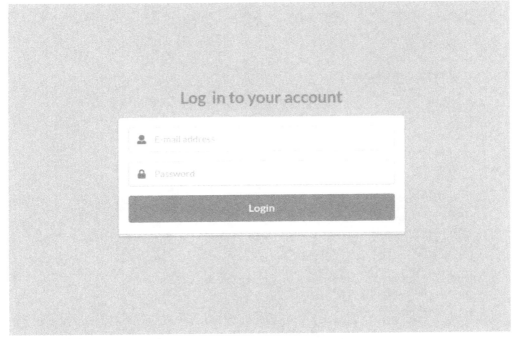

4-1. The login form component

If authentication succeeds, we call *this.$router.push()* to navigate to our intended route. If it fails, we set an error flag in order to render a message under the login form.

---

[5.] https://semantic-ui.com/usage/layout.html

Now that we have our authentication service and a way to ask for credentials, we need to secure the routes that un-authenticated users (guests) shouldn't have access to.

**src/router.js**

```javascript
import Vue from 'vue';
import Router from 'vue-router';
import authAPI from './auth';

import Home from './views/Home';
import Login from './views/Login';
import Users from './views/Users';

Vue.use(Router);

const router = new Router({
  mode: 'history',
  routes: [
    {
      path: '/',
      name: 'home',
      component: Home,
    },
    {
      path: '/login',
      component: Login,
    },
    {
      name: 'user',
      path: '/users/:userId',
      component: Users,
      beforeEnter: (to, from, next) => {
        if (authAPI.isAuthenticated() === false) {
          next('/login');
        } else {
          next();
        }
      },
    },
  ],
});
```

```
export default router;
```

At the top of the file, we're importing the auth service so we have a way to check the authentication status of the current user.

For the routes we want to protect, we need to assign a *beforeEnter* guard. The guard checks if the user is logged in and, if not, redirects to the */login* route.

Let's create the component for the Users page.

**views/Users.vue**

```
<template>
  <div>
    <h1>Users</h1>
    <p>Current route: {{ url }}</p>
    <ul>
      <li v-for="i in [1, 2, 3, 4, 5]" :key="i">
        <router-link :to="{ name: 'user', params: { userId: i } }"
          >User {{ i }}</router-link
        >
      </li>
    </ul>
  </div>
</template>

<script>
export default {
  name: "Users",
  data: () => ({
    url: null
  }),
  beforeRouteEnter(to, from, next) {
    next(component => (component.url = to.path));
  },
  beforeRouteUpdate(to, from, next) {
    this.url = to.path;
    next();
  }
```

```
  };
  </script>
```

If you've been following along with the book so far, everything here should be pretty straightforward. We have two route guards that update the page with the value of the current route path.

We also need to create a home page for the example, which will be accessible to guest users (that is, those who aren't authenticated).

**views/Home.vue**

```
<template>
  <div id="app">
    <h1 class="ui center aligned header">Welcome</h1>
    <router-link to="/users/1">Go to Users page</router-link>
  </div>
</template>

<script>
export default {
  name: "HomePage"
};
</script>
```

The *App.vue* component will be identical to the one from the example at the beginning of the chapter, so copy that into your project, and don't forget to install *semantic-ui-css* via npm.

If you're following along with the example on your own computer, you should now be able to launch the dev server by running *npm run serve* and view your app at *http://localhost:8080* .

 **Online Demo**

You can check out the online demo of this example on <u>CodeSandbox</u>[6].

---

[6.] https://codesandbox.io/s/9y2rkmn174

# Summary

In this chapter, I introduced Vue's official routing solution, Vue Router, and walked you through installing and configuring it to work with a Vue application.

We looked at all the main concepts you need to understand in order to start using Vue Router in your own applications, including how to create routes and navigate between them.

We also looked at what navigation guards are, and the different kinds that are available at a global, per-route, and per-component level. Lastly, we built upon some of this knowledge to create a basic app with protected routes for authenticated users only.

Chapter

# State Management

# 5

As an application gets larger and more complex, you start to run into situations where a given piece of state needs to be used in multiple components. **State** can be information that your app works with—for example, the details of the logged-in user, or the current "state" of some parts of the UI, such as whether a particular piece of functionality is disabled or data is being loaded.

A common solution is to "lift" that piece of state out of the component where it's being used and into the nearest parent. This can work fine when the components are close siblings, and the state doesn't reside too far up the tree, but otherwise can lead to what's called "prop drilling"—having to pass down props through several layers of components that don't need them themselves.

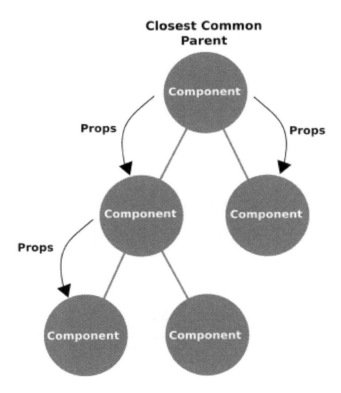

5-1. Lifting state into a parent component

Fortunately, many popular frameworks have tools that help to manage state.

You've most likely heard of Redux, a state management system popular in the React community. Vue also has its own official solution, called Vuex. Both of these systems work by having a central store for shared state, and mechanisms for giving access to pieces of that state to any component in your application tree.

In addition, they provide a centralized means to update that state. If different parts of an application can just change the shared state at random, it can lead to hard-to-trace bugs and inconsistencies. Having all changes go via the central store makes the app easier to reason about, and facilitates debugging tools that can log and replay changes to the state.

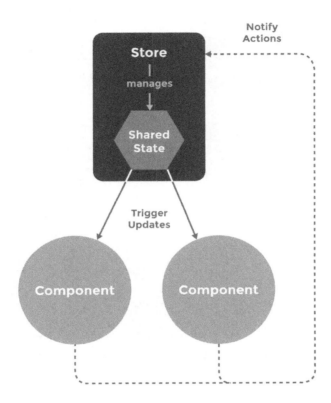

5-2. Vuex Data Flow

# Installing Vuex

As with the previous chapter, let's walk through installing Vuex into a fresh project.

Assuming we're starting with a new CLI-generated project (using the "default" preset), let's first install the Vuex library from npm:

```
npm install vuex
```

Once this has finished downloading, we'll need to register Vuex with Vue as a plugin and export a new store instance.

Let's create a new file, *store.js* , inside the *src* folder.

**src/store.js**

```
import Vue from "vue";
import Vuex from "vuex";

Vue.use(Vuex);

export default new Vuex.Store({
  state: {},
  mutations: {},
  actions: {}
});
```

We're passing the *Vuex.Store* constructor an object with three keys: *state* , *mutations* , and *actions* . Don't worry about these for now, as we'll go into each one in the next section.

We need to pass this new store object as an option when we create our main Vue instance, so let's open up *main.js* .

**src/main.js**

```
import Vue from "vue";
import App from "./App.vue";
import store from "./store";

Vue.config.productionTip = false;

new Vue({
  store,
  render: h => h(App)
```

```
}).$mount("#app");
```

As we did with the router in the last chapter, we import our newly created store and pass it to our Vue instance.

By registering the Vuex plugin and passing in a store instance, that store will be made available to every component in our application as `this.$store`.

 **Saving time with Vue CLI**

> As you may already have guessed, if you opt to install Vuex from the Vue CLI, this initial setup will be generated automatically.

## Basic Concepts

Now that we have a Vue project with Vuex wired up, let's take a look at the basic concepts of the library.

### State

The store's **state** is where all the data you're managing with Vuex lives. All the other functionality of the library revolves around accessing and updating this data.

The state itself is a single JavaScript object, on which you create properties to hold any data that needs to be shared between different components in your application:

```
export default new Vuex.Store({
  state: {
    customerName: 'John Smith',
    shoppingCart: [
      {
        name: 'Jumbo Box of Teabags',
        quantity: 1,
```

```
        price: 350
      },
      {
        name: 'Packet of Fancy Biscuits',
        quantity: 1,
        price: 199
      },
    ]
  },
});
```

State properties can contain any valid datatype, from booleans, to arrays, to other objects.

We can access the state in components where we want to use it by creating computed properties:

```
<template>
  <div>
    <span>{{ customerName }}</span>
  </div>
</template>

<script>
export default {
  computed: {
    customerName() {
      return this.$store.state.customerName;
    }
  }
}
</script>
```

In this example, the component is accessing the customer name from the store.

Vuex also provides a helper function for accessing the store's state, to cut down on the boilerplate.

**With the mapState helper**

```
<template>
  <div>
    <span>{{ customerName }}</span>
  </div>
</template>

<script>
import { mapState } from "vuex";

export default {
  computed: {
    ...mapState(['customerName'])
  }
}
</script>
```

The `mapState()` helper generates computed properties for us from a list of state property names. Notice that we're using object destructuring: the helpler returns an object of computed properties, so by destructuring these we can easily declare our own properties alongside the helper-generated ones.

## Getters

**Getters** are essentially a Vuex store's computed properties. They allow you to create *derived state* that can be shared between different components. Like a component's computed properties, the output from a getter is cached and only recalculated when the state it depends upon is updated:

```
export default new Vuex.Store({
  state: {
    shoppingCart: [
      // ...
    ]
  },
  getters: {
    cartItemCount: state => state.shoppingCart.length
  }
});
```

In the example above, we've got a getter called `cartItemCount` that returns the number of items in the user's shopping cart.

As when accessing the store state, to use this getter from within a component we need to create a computed property:

```
<template>
  <div>
    <span>Shopping Cart ({{ cartItemCount }} items)</span>
  </div>
</template>

<script>
export default {
  computed: {
    cartItemCount() {
      return this.$store.getters.cartItemCount;
    }
  }
}
</script>
```

Vuex provides a *mapGetters()* helper to eliminate some of the boilerplate:

```
<template>
  <div>
    <span>Shopping Cart ({{ cartItemCount }} items)</span>
  </div>
</template>

<script>
import { mapGetters } from "vuex";

export default {
  computed: {
    ...mapGetters(['cartItemCount'])
  }
}
</script>
```

## Mutations

One of the main problems with having shared global state in a program is that it can lead to problems that are very hard to debug. Since changes to the state could be coming literally from anywhere in the application, tracking down exactly when and where the state is mutated becomes very difficult.

The Vuex architecture deals with this problem by stating that components never change (or "mutate") the state directly. Instead, when we want to update the state in some way, we need to use a **mutation**.

By requiring all state changes to be made via mutations, Vuex can keep track of them. This enables tools like the Vue devtools to present a log of all the mutations applied to the store, allowing you to see exactly what changes were made and when.

If you've ever used Redux, a mutation occupies a similar role to a reducer. It takes the existing state and applies changes to it:

```
export default new Vuex.Store({
  state: {
    customerName: 'Fred'
  },
  mutations: {
    setCustomerName(state, name) {
      state.customerName = name;
    }
  }
});
```

The code above shows a mutation that changes the `customerName` state. To use a mutation, it has to be **committed** to the store using the `commit()` method of the store:

```
<template>
  <div>
    <p>{{ customerName }}</p>
```

```
    <input type="text" @input="updateName" :value="customerName" />
  </div>
</template>

<script>
import { mapState } from "vuex";

export default {
  name: "Example",
  computed: {
    ...mapState(['customerName'])
  },
  methods: {
    updateName(event) {
      this.$store.commit('setCustomerName', event.target.value);
    }
  }
}
</script>
```

In the example component above, the `customerName` state is displayed on the page and in an input control. If the input is changed, the store is updated via the mutation.

 **Live Demo**

You can try this example live on CodeSandbox[1].

As you might have guessed, there's a `mapMutations` helper available:

```
import { mapState, mapMutations } from 'vuex';

export default {
  name: "Example",
  computed: {
    ...mapState(['customerName'])
  },
```

---

[1.] https://codesandbox.io/s/j2r2950zz3

```
  methods: {
    ...mapMutations(['setCustomerName']),
    updateName(event) {
      this.setCustomerName(event.target.value);
    }
  }
}
```

In this example, we need to extract some data from the *event* object to send as the mutation's payload, so we end up having to create an additional method.

You'll notice that store state is reactive, like instance/component data is. This means that, as soon as a mutation is committed to the store, the changes flow down to your components automatically.

In order for Vuex to effectively keep track of how and when the state is mutated, mutations themselves *must* be synchronous. So what do we do when we need to run asynchronous code, such as making Ajax requests? That's where actions come in.

## Actions

To perform asynchronous tasks and/or commit multiple related mutations, we need actions. **Actions** are functions that *never* change state themselves, but rather delegate to mutations after performing some logic. They receive a *context* object as their first argument, which contains the keys *state*, *commit*, and *getters*.

As you might guess, *state* is the store's state tree, *commit* is the method for committing mutations to the store, and *getters* is a collection of all the getters that are defined in the store.

A typical action might do something like fetch some data from a remote API:

```
import Vue from "vue";
import Vuex from "vuex";
```

```
import axios from "axios";

Vue.use(Vuex);

export default new Vuex.Store({
  state: {
    users: [],
    isLoading: false,
  },
  mutations: {
    setLoadingTrue(state) {
      state.isLoading = true;
    },
    setLoadingFalse(state) {
      state.isLoading = false;
    },
    setUsers(state, users) {
      state.users = users;
    },
    setCustomerName(state, name) {
      state.customerName = name;
    }
  },
  actions: {
    getUsers(context) {
      context.commit('setLoadingTrue');
      axios.get('/api/users')
        .then(response => {
          context.commit('setUsers', response.data);
          context.commit('setLoadingFalse');
        })
        .catch(error => {
          context.commit('setLoadingFalse');
          // handle error
        });
    }
  }
});
```

Here, the *getUsers* action commits a mutation to set the *isLoading* state to *true*, and then makes an HTTP request to an API for a list of users. If the request is successful, two mutations are committed to set *isLoading* back to *false*, and to add the returned users collection to the store state.

If the request fails, the code toggles *isLoading* and may do some sort of error handling (for example, committing the error message to state, so it can be displayed somewhere in the app).

Like mutations, actions can't be called directly. Instead, actions are "dispatched" via a dedicated method on the store, *store.dispatch()*. Although this can be done from within any component by calling *this.$store.dispatch()*, it's usually more convenient to use the *mapActions()* helper:

```
<template>
  <div>
    <div id="spinner" v-if="isLoading">
      <img src="spinner.gif" />
    </div>
    <ul v-else>
      <li v-for="(user, index) in users" :key="index" >{{ user }}</li>
    </ul>
  </div>
</template>

<script>
import { mapActions, mapState } from "vuex";

export default {
  computed: {
    ...mapState([
      'isLoading',
      'users'
    ])
  },
  methods: {
    ...mapActions(['getUsers'])
  },
  created() {
    this.getUsers();
  }
}
</script>
```

In this example, we're calling the *getUsers* action from the component's *created()* lifecycle hook. As soon as we do, the *isLoading* state is updated, and the spinner is displayed. Once the Ajax request has completed, the state is updated again, hiding the spinner and displaying the returned users.

# Example

To finish, let's tie all of these concepts together and add Vuex functionality to our employee directory.

We'll start off by generating a fresh Vue project with the CLI, and opt to manually select features. In addition to the defaults, we want to check the options for Vue Router and Vuex.

With our fresh project, let's alter the index page first of all to add some markup and CSS for the demo.

**public/index.html**

```html
<!DOCTYPE html>
<html>
  <head>
    <meta charset="utf-8" />
    <meta http-equiv="X-UA-Compatible" content="IE=edge,chrome=1" />
    <meta name="viewport"
    content="width=device-width, initial-scale=1.0, maximum-scale=1.0">
    <title>Vuex Example - Jump Start Vue.js</title>
    <link rel="stylesheet" type="text/css"
    href="https://cdnjs.cloudflare.com/ajax/libs/semantic-ui/2.3.1/semantic.min.css">

    <style type="text/css">
      body {
        background-color: #FFFFFF;
      }
      .ui.menu .item img.logo {
        margin-right: 1.5em;
      }
      .main.container {
        margin-top: 7em;
      }
    </style>
```

```
    </head>
    <body>
      <div id="app"></div>
    </body>
  </html>
```

Nothing revolutionary here: just a CDN link to the Semantic UI library, and some additional styling tweaks.

Let's follow this up by altering the  *<App>*  component.

**src/App.vue**

```
<template>
  <div>
    <div class="ui fixed inverted menu">
      <div class="ui container">
        <div class="header item">
          <img class="logo" src="./assets/logo.png">
          Jump Start Vue.js
        </div>
        <router-link class="item" to="/" exact>Home</router-link>
        <router-link class="item" to="/users">Users</router-link>
      </div>
    </div>
    <router-view></router-view>
  </div>
</template>

<script>
import { mapActions } from "vuex";

export default {
  name: "App",
  methods: {
    ...mapActions(["fetchUsers"])
  },
  created() {
    this.fetchUsers();
  }
};
```

```
    </script>
```

You'll notice some `<router-link>` components in the menu, which allow navigating between the pages we're going to create. The other thing of note in this component is that we're mapping a `fetchUsers` action from our store, and we're calling that as soon as the component is created.

Let's take a look at the store itself next.

**src/store.js**

```
import Vue from "vue";
import Vuex from "vuex";
import axios from "axios";

Vue.use(Vuex);

export default new Vuex.Store({
  state: {
    users: [],
    selectedUserId: null,
    isFetching: false
  },
  mutations: {
    setUsers(state, { users }) {
      state.users = users;
    },
    setSelectedUser(state, id) {
      state.selectedUserId = id;
    },
    setIsFetching(state, bool) {
      state.isFetching = bool;
    }
  },
  getters: {
    selectedUser: state =>
      state.users.find(user => user.login.uuid === state.selectedUserId)
  },
  actions: {
    fetchUsers({ commit }) {
```

```
      commit("setIsFetching", true);
      return axios
        .get("https://randomuser.me/api/?nat=gb,us,au&results=5&seed=abc")
        .then(res => {
          setTimeout(() => {
            commit("setIsFetching", false);
            commit("setUsers", { users: res.data.results });
          }, 2500);
        })
        .catch(error => {
          commit("setIsFetching", false);
          console.error(error);
        });
    }
  }
});
```

Hopefully, if you've been following along with the chapter so far, the above code should be fairly self explanatory. We're including the <u>axios</u>[2] library in order to fetch some dummy data from a remote API. There's also a small timeout before returning the results to simulate network latency and demonstrate the loading state.

 **Installing axios**

> In order to build the example, you'll need to install axios via npm:

```
npm install axios
```

Next, we have three page components: Home, Users, and User.

**src/views/Home.vue**

```
<template>
  <div class="ui main text container">
    <h1 class="ui header">Chapter 5: State Management</h1>
```

---

[2.] https://github.com/axios/axios

```
    <p>This is a basic Vuex example app, to demo the concepts learned in the
    ↪accompanying chapter.</p>
    <p>Go to <router-link to="/users">Users</router-link></p>
  </div>
</template>

<script>
export default {
  name: "Home"
}
</script>
```

There's nothing exciting going on here, but we're including a link to our */users* route that we'll set up shortly.

### src/views/Users.vue

```
<template>
  <div class="ui main text container">
    <h1 class="ui header">Users</h1>
    <div class="ui active inverted dimmer" v-if="isFetching">
      <div class="ui text loader">Loading</div>
    </div>
    <ul v-else>
      <li v-for="(user, index) in users" :key="index">
        <router-link :to="{ name: 'user', params: { id: user.login.uuid }}">
          {{ user.name.title }} {{ user.name.first }} {{ user.name.last }}
        </router-link>
      </li>
    </ul>
  </div>
</template>

<script>
import { mapState } from "vuex";

export default {
  name: "Users",
  computed: {
    ...mapState([
      'isFetching',
```

```
      'users'
    ])
  }
}
</script>

<style>
  li {
    text-transform: capitalize;
  }
</style>
```

In this component, we're mapping two pieces of state: *isFetching* , and *users* .
The first is used to display a loading spinner to the user while the users are being
fetched from the remote API. The second is the collection of users itself, which
we're iterating over and display as a list of names with links to a dedicated URL
for each.

### src/views/User.vue

```
<template>
  <div class="ui main text container" v-if="selectedUser">
    <div class="ui items">
      <div class="item">
        <div class="image">
          <img :src="selectedUser.picture.large">
        </div>
        <div class="content">
          <a class="header">{{ fullName }}</a>
          <div class="meta">
            <span>{{ selectedUser.email }}</span>
          </div>
          <div class="description">
            <p>{{ selectedUser.location.street }}, {{ selectedUser.location.city }},
            {{ selectedUser.location.state }}, {{ selectedUser.location.postcode }}
            </p>
          </div>
          <div class="extra">
            {{ selectedUser.phone }}<br />
            {{ selectedUser.cell }}
          </div>
```

```
        </div>
      </div>
    </div>
  </div>
</template>

<script>
import { mapGetters, mapMutations } from "vuex";

export default {
  name: "Users",
  computed: {
    ...mapGetters(["selectedUser"]),
    fullName() {
      return `${this.selectedUser.name.first} ${this.selectedUser.name.last}`;
    }
  },
  methods: {
    ...mapMutations(["setSelectedUser"])
  },
  created() {
    const userId = this.$route.params.id;
    this.setSelectedUser(userId);
  }
};
</script>

<style scoped>
  a.header, p {
    text-transform: capitalize;
  }
</style>
```

This component displays more details about an individual user. It works by getting the user's ID from the route when the component is created, and committing this to the store via a mutation. This causes the *selectedUser* getter to update, rendering the component with the chosen user's details.

Let's now create some routes for these components.

**src/router.js**

```
import Vue from "vue";
import Router from "vue-router";

import Home from "./views/Home.vue";
import Users from "./views/Users.vue";
import User from "./views/User.vue";

Vue.use(Router);

export default new Router({
  mode: "history",
  linkActiveClass: "active",
  routes: [
    {
      path: "/",
      name: "home",
      component: Home
    },
    {
      name: "users",
      path: "/users",
      component: Users
    },
    {
      name: "user",
      path: "/users/:id",
      component: User
    }
  ]
});
```

If you read the previous chapter, there should be nothing to surprise you here. The `linkActiveClass` option is set, so that the correct class is applied to active links for Semantic UI to style.

 **Online Demo**

You can experiment with this example online at CodeSandbox[3].

---

3. https://codesandbox.io/s/200x60vkoy

## Summary

In this chapter, we looked at what state management solutions are and what problems they help to solve. Let's recap what we've learned:

- The state is a single JavaScript object holding any data that needs to be shared between components in your application. We can access the state in components by creating computed properties, or by using the `mapState` helper function.
- Getters are essentially a Vuex store's computed properties. They allow you to create *derived state* that can be shared between different components. To use a getter from within a component, we need to create a computed property, or use the `mapGetters()` helper.
- Components never change (or "mutate") the state directly. When we want to update the state in some way, we need to use a *mutation*. To use a mutation, it has to be *committed* to the store using the `commit()` method. You can also use the `mapMutations` helper. Mutations must always be synchronous.
- Actions are functions that *never* change state themselves, but rather delegate to mutations after performing some logic (often asynchronous). They receive a `context` object as their first argument, which contains the keys `state`, `commit`, and `getters`. Like mutations, actions aren't called directly. Instead, actions are *dispatched* via a dedicated method on the store, `store.dispatch()`. Although this can be done from within any component by calling `this.$store.dispatch()`, it's usually more convenient to use the `mapActions()` helper.

Nuxt.js

# 6

While Vue.js is frequently referred to as a framework, out of the box it doesn't come with all the functionality you might need to build more sophisticated web applications, such as routing and state management.

Nuxt.js (hereafter referred to as Nuxt) is a non-official framework that brings together Vue, Vue Router, and Vuex, and was inspired by the similar, React-based framework Next.js[1]. It takes a convention-over-configuration approach to remove a lot of the boilerplate from the process of developing Vue applications.

With some frameworks, this approach can become restrictive when you want to venture beyond the use cases the developers had in mind. Nuxt's conventions reduce the time it takes to build out sophisticated Vue applications, but almost every aspect of the framework can be overridden, tweaked, and customized.

Although that in itself is an attractive proposition, Nuxt's killer feature is its support for server-side rendering[2] (SSR). As you're probably aware, creating JavaScript apps that can be rendered on the server as well as on the client (often referred to as universal web applications[3]) is a very useful technique for improving first-load performance and SEO.

SSR is commonly quite a complicated thing to put in place, so Nuxt really scores here by making the process relatively straightforward and painless. As if that wasn't enough, it now supports static site generation as well, allowing you to get the performance and SEO benefits of SSR on cheap, static-page hosting.

## Starting a Nuxt Project

While it's possible to manually install and configure Nuxt, it has its own installation tool which does the initial configuration for you and provides you with a skeleton application layout to get you started.

You can start the installation process by running the following command

---

[1]. https://nextjs.org/
[2]. https://vuejs.org/v2/guide/ssr.html
[3]. http://www.acuriousanimal.com/2016/08/10/universal-applications.html

(assuming you have npm 5.2.0+ installed):

```
npx create-nuxt-app <project-name>
```

The *npx* command is a handy npm utility that will load and run the installer without the need to install the module into your global *node_modules* folder first.

 **Installing with Yarn**

It's also possible to run the installer via Yarn, with the following command:

```
yarn create nuxt-app <my-project>
```

Once the installer downloads, it will prompt you with a series of options for your new project, in a very similar manner to the Vue CLI.

You'll be given the following options:

- **Project Name**. The default is the name you provided for the project folder, but you can override this here if you wish.
- **Description**. A description for your project. Both this and the project name are used to fill in the *package.json* file.
- **Use a custom server framework**. By default, Nuxt hides the server functionality out of sight, but it's possible to choose from a handful of Node frameworks and have it use that instead. You can pick from Express, Koa, Hapi, Feathers, Micro, and Adonis. You probably won't want this option unless you have a specific need to customize the server-side functionality.
- **Use a custom UI framework**. You can also choose between a handful of CSS UI frameworks in order to have one pre-configured for you. You can pick from Bootstrap[4], Vuetify[5], Bulma[6], Tailwind[7], Element UI[8], Ant Design Vue[9], and

---

[4.] https://github.com/bootstrap-vue/bootstrap-vue
[5.] https://github.com/vuetifyjs/vuetify
[6.] https://github.com/jgthms/bulma

Buefy[10]. These are convenient if you want to use one of the given frameworks, but it's easy enough to add your own later.

- **Rendering mode**. Nuxt offers you the choice between a standard SPA (single page application), or a universal web app, which pre-renders each request on the server for better performance and SEO. While Nuxt's conventions and structure can still be useful for building SPAs, its main selling point is the SSR/static site generation. Hence, "universal" is the default here.
- **axios module**. This module wraps the axios HTTP library and gives it better integration with Nuxt. You don't have to use it, but it's recommended.
- **ESLint**. Pre-installs ESLint for you.
- **Prettier**. Pre-installs Prettier.
- **Author name**. Your name, for the `package.json` file.
- **Package manager**. You can choose from npm or Yarn to have Nuxt configure itself for your chosen package manager.

If you're intending to follow along with the examples in this chapter, then accept all the default options except for the axios module, which you should say "yes" to.

Once you've answered all the questions, Nuxt will go ahead and download the necessary dependencies, and create a basic folder layout with some boilerplate code. At the time of writing, some of these files will cause linting errors (if you have ESLint and Prettier installed) which you can fix by running `npm run lint --fix` or `yarn run lint --fix`.

 **Source Control**

As part of the install process, Nuxt will initialize your new project folder as a Git repo. However, unlike the Vue CLI, it won't make the initial commit for you. It's a good idea to do this as your first step!

To get started building your app with Nuxt, spin up the built-in development

---

7. https://github.com/tailwindcss/tailwindcss
8. https://github.com/ElemeFE/element
9. https://github.com/vueComponent/ant-design-vue
10. https://buefy.github.io/

server:

```
npm run dev
```

While this process is running, it will automatically rebuild your app if it detects any changes. Let's take a look at the folder structure that Nuxt uses.

# Project Layout

Below is the default folder structure that the Nuxt installer leaves you with. There's a *README* file inside each directory, but I've left those off for clarity.

```
├── assets
├── components
│   └── Logo.vue
├── layouts
│   └── default.vue
├── middleware
├── pages
│   └── index.vue
├── plugins
├── static
│   └── favicon.ico
├── store
├── nuxt.config.js
├── package.json
└── package-lock.json
```

Let's look at each of these folders and see what role they play within a Nuxt application.

## pages

As I mentioned at the beginning of the chapter, Nuxt favors convention over configuration. Rather than having to create a router configuration and specify all your app's routes and the components they map to, Nuxt can do the hard work for you.

Any components you place inside the *pages* folder will automatically be wired up according to a simple set of conventions.

Placing a component named *about.vue* into the folder will automatically create the route */about* in your app. Likewise, putting components within subfolders will add the respective segments to the route, so *user/profile.vue* would give you a URL of */user/profile* .

What about creating routes with dynamic segments? There's a simple rule for that too. Let's say we want to recreate the blog route we looked at in <u>Chapter 4</u>, */blog/:slug* . We would create a *blog* subfolder within *pages* , and inside that create the file *_slug.vue* . Beginning the name with an underscore lets Nuxt know this segment of the route will be dynamic.

This is equivalent to creating the following route config:

```
{
  name: 'blog-slug',
  path: '/blog/:slug',
  component: 'pages/blog/_slug.vue'
}
```

The installer also creates a *components* folder for any other Vue components that you don't want to affect the routing configuration.

## layouts

In previous chapters, we put any markup that was common to every "page" of our app into the *<App>* component. But this isn't a very flexible approach. What if we wanted to have different layouts for different sections of our app?

Fortunately, Nuxt provides us with a neat solution to this. The *layouts* folder contains a component called *default.vue* , which contains the following markup.

**layouts/default.vue**

```
<template>
  <div>
    <nuxt/>
  </div>
</template>

<style>
  ...
</style>
```

The important thing to note here is the `<nuxt/>` component. This is Nuxt's equivalent of the `<router-view>` component we saw in <u>Chapter 4</u>, and it's necessary in order for your app's components to actually be displayed. As you can see, this layout simply renders the page component within a plain `<div>`.

To change the layout, we just need to create a new file in the layouts directory (for example, `two-column.vue`) and specify that we want to use this layout for a page component by adding a `layout` property to its options.

**pages/faq.vue**

```
<script>
  export default {
    layout: 'two-column'
  }
</script>
```

 **Avoid Styling Global Markup**

At the time of writing, there's a bug in Nuxt which results in CSS rules from a layout component remaining in the page even after navigating to pages using a different layout. For this reason, avoid styling global elements (such as the `<body>` tag) from within your layouts.

## assets

The `assets` folder is for any non-JS assets (such as images, fonts and CSS files) that you want to use from your components. You can access the contents of this folder via the `~` alias, both within your components' code *and* template sections.

So, for example, if you have the file `logo.png` that you want to use in one of your components, you can put the file in the `assets` folder and reference it within your component template like this:

```
<img src="~/assets/logo.png">
```

 **Inlining Smaller Assets**

> By default, Nuxt configures webpack (which it uses under the hood to bundle your application) to convert any images and fonts smaller than 1KB to inline base-64 data URLs.

For other kinds of assets that you don't want to be processed by webpack, Nuxt creates the `static` folder. Files in this folder will be served relative to the app's base URL, so `static/brochure.pdf` will be available as `/brochure.pdf` .

## store

There's no Vuex store set up by default with Nuxt, but it's very easy to add one should your app require it. All that's necessary for a basic store is to create an `index.js` file within the `store` folder.

 **Reloading the Development Server**

> If you add a Vuex store to your Nuxt application, you'll need to restart the development server before you can access it from your components!

Defining the store is slightly different than in a non-Nuxt app: the store file needs to return a factory function that will return a new store when called.

**store/index.js**

```
import Vuex from 'vuex'

export default () => {
  return new Vuex.Store({
    state: () => ({
      // ...
    }),
    mutations: {
      // ...
    }
  })
}
```

It's also important to note that the `state` property must be a function that returns the base state object. This is to prevent problems with shared state when the site is rendered on the server.

The store can also define a special action, `nuxtServerInit`, which will be called whenever a page is rendered on the server:

```
actions: {
  nuxtServerInit ({ commit }, { req, res }) {
    // ...
  }
}
```

As well as the usual Vuex context object that actions receive, this method receives a Nuxt context object as its second argument.

This object contains quite a lot of keys (see the API documentation[11] for a full list), including the server request and response objects— `req` and `res` respectively. This allows you to pre-populate the store with the logged-in user, for

---

11. https://nuxtjs.org/api/context

example.

## middleware

This folder is for code that you want to be run for every page, or a group of pages. To create a middleware, you add a `.js` file that exports a function. When the function is called, it'll be passed a context object.

Middleware can be used to do things like check the authentication status of the current user.

**middleware/authenticated.js**

```
export default function ({ store, redirect }) {
  if (!store.getters.isAuthenticated) {
    return redirect('/login')
  }
}
```

The example middleware shown above uses a Vuex getter to check if the user is authenticated, and if not, redirects them to the login page.

To use a middleware, you add a `middleware` property to a page or layout component. This property is a string (or an array of strings) containing the name of the middleware(s) that you want to run before the component is loaded.

**layouts/admin.vue**

```
export default {
  middleware: 'authenticated'
}
```

## plugins

Because Nuxt abstracts away the underlying setup of Vue and libraries like Vue Router, you might be wondering how to install other Vue plugins.

The Nuxt way of handling this is to create a file inside the *plugins* folder where you do the usual initialization.

**plugins/vue-flash-message.js**

```
import Vue from 'vue';
import VueFlashMessage from 'vue-flash-message';

Vue.use(VueFlashMessage);
```

Then tell Nuxt about the plugin, by editing the *plugins* key of the global config file.

**nuxt.config.js**

```
export default {
  // ...
  plugins: [
    { src: '~/plugins/vue-flash-message', ssr: false }
  ],
  // ...
}
```

Note that, in the example above, we're setting the *ssr* property to false to prevent the code being executed on the server. Many Vue plugins aren't written with SSR in mind and can crash Nuxt if they try to access browser-only globals.

## Nuxt Component Options

In order to hook into the functionality that the framework offers, Nuxt allows you to add some specific properties and functions to your page components. Let's take a look at them.

### asyncData

Before a component is initialized, Nuxt will look to see if it has an *asyncData* method. If it does, this method is called, giving you the opportunity to fetch any data you might need to render the component.

On the initial request it will be run on the server, but once the app has loaded, subsequent calls will be run on the client as the user navigates around the running SPA.

The method receives the Nuxt context object as its first parameter. This object gives you access to the following.

- **app**. The main Vue instance for your application, including any attached plugins.
- **route**. The current route object (see <u>Chapter 4</u>).
- **store**. The Vuex store, if you're using one.
- **params**. A shortcut to the `route.params` object.
- **query**. A shortcut to the `route.query` object.
- **req**. The request object (if running on the server).
- **res**. The response object (if running on the server).
- **redirect**. A function for redirecting the current route.
- **error**. A function for displaying an error page.

 **Additional Context Properties**

> See the documentation for <u>an exhaustive list of additional properties</u>[12].

The return value from the method should be an object that Nuxt can merge with the component's `data` object. It's important to note that you *don't* have access to the component itself from within the `asyncData` method, as it hasn't yet been initialized.

```
asyncData ({ $axios, params, error }) {
  return $axios.get(`https://api.mysite.com/posts/${params.slug}`)
    .then(res => ({ content: res.data }))
```

---

12. https://nuxtjs.org/api/context

```
      .catch(e => error({ statusCode: 404, message: 'Post not found' }))
  }
```

In the example above, we fetch the slug (which is a route parameter) from the context object and use it to request the content from an API.

If the request is successful, the content is returned and Nuxt will merge it into our page's data. If it fails, we call the `error` method, passing it an object with a `statusCode` and a `message` key.

## fetch

The `fetch` method is very similar to `asyncData`, except that it doesn't merge returned data into your component. Rather, the purpose of this method is to allow you to populate your Vuex store.

You can fetch the data directly within this method and commit it to the store, or you can opt to dispatch an action in your store that takes care of fetching the data itself.

Like `asyncData`, this method receives the context object, allowing you access to the store state, getters, and `dispatch` and `commit` functions.

## head

The `head` property allows you to set options for the page header and metadata:

```
{
  title: 'About Us',
  meta: [
    { name: 'description',
      content: 'Spacely Sprockets is the galaxy\'s largest producer ...' }
  ]
}
```

These properties will be output in the header when the page is rendered.

### layout

As mentioned in the earlier section on layouts, setting this property allows you to change which layout the page component will be rendered within.

# Building for Production

Once we have our new site or application built with Nuxt, the next step is to run the build process and prepare our code to be deployed.

## Single Page Application

If you chose the SPA mode when creating the project (or if you changed the `mode` setting in `nuxt.config.js` ) you can build your code as a normal front-end app.

Running the command `npm run build` will generate your app inside the `dist` folder, allowing you to deploy it to your web hosting.

## Universal Application

For SSR apps, we need to copy our project folder to a web server and first run the `npm run build` command. Once the application code has been built, we can run `npm run start` to launch the Nuxt server.

By default, the server runs on port 3000 (although this can be set in `nuxt.config.js` ) so you'll need to configure your web server to proxy incoming requests to the app.

The Nuxt FAQ site <u>provides examples</u>[13] of configuring a NGINX proxy, as well as deploying a Nuxt app to popular platforms.

---

[13.] https://nuxtjs.org/faq/nginx-proxy

## Static Site

Static site generation attempts to be the best of both worlds.

In a universal app, the initially requested page is rendered on the server and returned to the browser, where the client-side code then takes over rendering the rest of the app as the user navigates around.

Static site generation, on the other hand, renders all possible routes in advance, saving the output as HTML files. This technique gives you the benefit of fast response times, and pages that are indexable by the search engines, without the overhead of running a Node.js server.

It's important to bear in mind your pages will only be as up to date as the last time you ran the generate command, making this approach more suited to situations where the data changes less often. For sites that rely on frequently changing data (for example, up-to-the-minute news or stock data), users (and search engine spiders) could potentially be seeing out-of-date information.

You can generate a static version of your site by running `npm run generate` and the resulting files will be saved to the `dist` folder.

There's one important thing to be aware of when generating sites with dynamic route segments. By default, these will be ignored by Nuxt, as it has no way of knowing all the possible parameter values the route could be called with.

To get around this problem, Nuxt allows you to give it a list of routes to render, adding them to `nuxt.config.js` as an array:

```
export default {
  // ...
  generate: {
    routes: [
      '/blog/my-first-post',
      '/blog/pictures-of-my-cat',
      '/blog/the-best-pie-ever'
```

```
    ]
   }
   // ...
  }
```

It's possible to generate the list of routes programmatically so you can do things like query an API endpoint for a current list of posts (for example). I recommend checking out the **official documentation**[14] if you want to know more.

## Summary

Hopefully this chapter has given you a good understanding of what Nuxt.js is and why you might want to use it. We started off by talking about how it brings together Vue, Vue Router, and Vuex, providing some straightforward conventions that allow you to quickly build apps with a minimum of boilerplate code.

We walked through the install process, and looked at the skeleton application structure that it creates, using this as a starting point to see how Nuxt applications are put together.

We saw how to implement SSR with Nuxt and looked at some of the properties and methods it makes available to facilitate this.

Lastly, we saw how to build a Nuxt app for production as either a plain SPA, or as a universal SSR app, and examined the pros and cons of the recent *generate* command and when we might want to use it.

---

[14.] https://nuxtjs.org/api/configuration-generate#routes

# Tying It All Together

Chapter

7

In this last chapter, I'd like to put what we learned from the previous chapter (and indeed the rest of the book) into practice by building out an example universal web app.

My intention is to create a basic application by building upon some of the examples we've looked at throughout the book. Following along and coding the demo yourself will help to reinforce what you've learned so far and give you confidence in applying these tools and techniques in your own projects.

The app we'll create will fetch data from a remote API and display it in a custom component on the home page. Clicking one of the items should take the user through to a detail page with more information.

 **The Completed App Code**

> The full code for the app we're creating in this chapter is <u>available on GitHub</u>[1].

## Creating a Nuxt App

Let's start off by creating a fresh project with the Nuxt installer:

```
npx create-nuxt-app staff-manager
```

When the installer starts prompting you for input, go with the defaults for all options except for "Use axios module", to which you should answer yes. axios is the request library we'll be using to make calls to a third-party API, and Nuxt's axios module makes it seamlessly available throughout the framework.

Once the installer finishes, let's change into the new project and commit the skeleton project to the empty Git repository that's been set up:

```
cd staff-manager
```

---

[1] https://github.com/spbooks/jsvuejs1/

```
git add .
git commit -m "Initial commit"
```

Now that we have a good base to build on, let's customize the default layout. At this stage, you might want to start the development server by running `npm run dev`, in order to see the changes as we go along.

## Setting Up the Layout

We're going to add the basic navbar menu that we saw in <u>Chapter 5</u>, as we want this to appear on every page of our app.

Open the default layout file from the layouts folder, and replace the contents with the following.

**layouts/default.vue**

```
<template>
  <div>
    <div class="ui fixed inverted menu">
      <div class="ui container">
        <a
          href="#"
          class="header item"
        >
          <img
            class="logo"
            src="~assets/logo.png"
          >
          Staff Manager
        </a>
        <nuxt-link
          class="item"
          to="/"
          exact
        >Home</nuxt-link>
        <nuxt-link
          class="item"
          to="/users"
```

```
        >Users</nuxt-link>
      </div>
    </div>
    <nuxt/>
  </div>
</template>

<style>
body {
  background-color: #ffffff;
}
.ui.menu .item img.logo {
  margin-right: 1.5em;
}
.main.container {
  margin-top: 7em;
}
</style>
```

The only real difference here from before is that we're using the `<nuxt-link>` components for our menu links. Note that the logo comes from the default Vue CLI project, but you can grab a copy from the GitHub repo I mentioned earlier.

In order to load the Semantic UI styles for our app, we'll have to edit the Nuxt config.

**nuxt.config.js**

```
// ...
head: {
  title: pkg.name,
  meta: [
    { charset: 'utf-8' },
    { name: 'viewport', content: 'width=device-width, initial-scale=1' },
    { hid: 'description', name: 'description', content: pkg.description }
  ],
  link: [
    { rel: 'icon', type: 'image/x-icon', href: '/favicon.ico' },
    {
      rel: 'stylesheet',
```

```
      type: 'text/css',
      href:
        'https://cdnjs.cloudflare.com/ajax/libs/semantic-ui/2.3.1/semantic.min.css'
    }
  ]
},
// ...
```

Here we're telling Nuxt about the CDN link that we want to be included in our global *<head>* section.

 **Specifying** <head> **Content**

> In addition to setting app-wide head content via the configuration file, it's also possible to do so on a per-layout and per-page-component basis, by adding a *<head>* property.

## Initializing a Vuex Store

We're going to set up a basic Vuex store to centralize the handling of the employee data.

Let's create the file *index.js* inside the store folder.

**store/index.js**

```
import Vuex from 'vuex';

const createStore = () => {
  return new Vuex.Store({
    state: () => ({
      employees: []
    }),

    getters: {},

    mutations: {},
```

```
    actions: {}
  })
};

export default createStore;
```

Our initial state consists of the key *employees*, which we're initializing as an empty array.

We need to add an action to retrieve the list of employees from our API:

```
actions: {
  async getEmployees({ commit }) {
    const { results } = await this.$axios.$get(
      'https://randomuser.me/api/?nat=gb,us,au&results=10&seed=abc'
    );
    commit('setEmployees', { employees: results });
  }
}
```

You might notice that we're using axios here without having to import it. One of the benefits that the Nuxt axios module gives us is being able to access the library as *this.$axios* within our store actions.

We also need to add a mutation to add the returned data to our state:

```
mutations: {
  setEmployees(state, { employees }) {
    state.employees = employees
  }
},
```

We need to be able to access the list of employees, and rather than just read from the state directly from within our components, we're going to add a getter:

```
getters: {
  employeeList(state) {
```

```
    return state.employees.map(member => ({
      id: member.login.uuid,
      firstName: member.name.first,
      lastName: member.name.last,
      email: member.email,
      phone: member.phone,
      nationality: member.nat,
      avatar: member.picture.thumbnail
    }));
  }
},
```

The reason for using a getter is that we can now map the employee records into a simpler format, with just the properties that we're going to need.

 **A Reminder about Vuex Concepts**

**Getters** are essentially a Vuex store's computed properties. They allow you to create derived state that can be shared between different components.

**Mutations** are what we use to update the store state in some way. Components never change (or "mutate") the state directly.

**Actions** are functions that delegate to mutations after performing some logic (often asynchronous).

## Adding the Users Page

The Users page is going to reuse the `<StaffDirectory>` component we built in Chapter 3 to display the list of employees.

We're going to modify the component slightly, so let's do that first by creating the file `StaffDirectory.vue` within the components folder.

**components/StaffDirectory.vue**

```
<template>
  <div class="ui container">
    <input
      v-model="filterBy"
      placeholder="Filter By Last Name"
    >
    <table class="ui celled table">
      <thead>
        <tr>
          <th>Photo</th>
          <th @click="sortBy = 'firstName'">First Name</th>
          <th @click="sortBy = 'lastName'">Last Name</th>
          <th @click="sortBy = 'email'">Email</th>
          <th @click="sortBy = 'phone'">Phone</th>
          <th @click="sortBy = 'nationality'">Nationality</th>
        </tr>
      </thead>
      <tbody>
        <tr
          v-for="(employee, index) in sortedEmployees"
          :key="index"
          @click="$emit('select', employee)"
        >
          <td>
            <img
              :src="employee.avatar"
              class="ui mini rounded image"
            >
          </td>
          <td class="capitalize">{{ employee.firstName }}</td>
          <td class="capitalize">{{ employee.lastName }}</td>
          <td>{{ employee.email }}</td>
          <td>{{ employee.phone }}</td>
          <td>{{ employee.nationality }}</td>
        </tr>
      </tbody>
      <tfoot>
        <tr>
          <th colspan="6">{{ sortedEmployees.length }} employees</th>
        </tr>
      </tfoot>
    </table>
  </div>
```

```
</template>

<script>
export default {
  name: 'StaffDirectory',
  props: {
    employees: {
      type: Array,
      default: () => []
    }
  },
  data() {
    return {
      sortBy: 'firstName',
      filterBy: ''
    };
  },
  computed: {
    sortedEmployees() {
      return this.employees
        .filter(employee => employee.lastName.includes(this.filterBy))
        .sort((a, b) => a[this.sortBy].localeCompare(b[this.sortBy]));
    }
  }
}
</script>

<style scoped>
h1.ui.center.header {
  margin-top: 3em;
}
th:not(:first-child):hover,
tbody tr {
  cursor: pointer;
}
input {
  padding: 3px;
}
.capitalize {
  text-transform: capitalize;
}
</style>
```

The main difference here from the version in **Chapter 3** is that this component accepts an array of employees as a prop. It also fires a *selected* event when a row is clicked, passing the employee object as the payload.

Next, we'll create the home page, where we'll display the staff directory. Create a folder, *users*, within the *pages* folder, and add the file *index.vue* inside it. This will correspond to the route */users/* .

**pages/users/index.vue**

```
<template>
  <div class="ui main text container">
    <h1 class="ui header">Users</h1>
    <StaffDirectory
      :employees="employeeList"
      @select="showDetail"
    />
  </div>
</template>

<script>
import { mapGetters } from 'vuex'
import StaffDirectory from '~/components/StaffDirectory'

export default {
  components: { StaffDirectory },
  fetch: ({ store }) => {
    return store.dispatch('getEmployees');
  },
  computed: {
    ...mapGetters(['employeeList'])
  },
  methods: {
    showDetail(employee) {
      this.$router.push({
        name: 'users-id',
        params: { id: employee.id }
      });
    }
  }
}
</script>
```

We're using the Nuxt-specific `fetch()` method here to dispatch our `getEmployees` action when the page is navigated to. As we saw in the previous chapter, this method is called before the page component is loaded, and gives us the opportunity to dispatch actions to our store.

Once the action has completed, the component receives the array of employees from the store via the getter we defined previously, and passes it to the `<StaffDirectory>` component as a prop.

In addition, we're listening on the directory component for the `select` event. When this fires, the page's `showDetail` method will programmatically change the route to an individual employee's detail view.

# Users

| Photo | First Name | Last Name | Email | Phone | Nationality |
|-------|-----------|-----------|-------|-------|-------------|
| | Aiden | Gray | aiden.gray@example.com | 015394 67142 | GB |
| | Caitlin | Gardner | caitlin.gardner@example.com | 015242 36891 | GB |
| | Jerome | Myers | jerome.myers@example.com | 06-3870-3785 | AU |
| | Karl | Neal | karl.neal@example.com | 00-7827-8844 | AU |
| | Kitty | Horton | kitty.horton@example.com | 07-9701-3525 | AU |
| | Loretta | Woods | loretta.woods@example.com | (362)-351-8980 | US |
| | Sarah | Watts | sarah.watts@example.com | 017684 88732 | GB |
| | Tanya | Jordan | tanya.jordan@example.com | (094)-360-2756 | US |
| | Tomothy | Clarke | tomothy.clarke@example.com | 017687 30345 | GB |
| | Zoe | Jacobs | zoe.jacobs@example.com | 017684 35658 | GB |

10 employees

7-1. The list of employees on the Users page

Let's create that view next.

## The Employee Detail View

Our detail view needs to get the ID from the route parameters, and dispatch an action to the store to select the chosen employee.

First, let's add this action to the store, to select the chosen employee record.

**store/index.js**

```
state: () => ({
  employees: [],
  selectedEmployee: null
}),
```

To start with, we need to initialize a property in the store's state:

```
actions: {
  async getEmployees({ commit }) { ... },

  async getEmployee({ commit, dispatch, state }, { id }) {
    if (state.employees.length === 0) {
      await dispatch('getEmployees');
    }

    const employee = state.employees.find(user => user.login.uuid === id);
    commit('setSelectedEmployee', { employee });
  }
}
```

Commonly, you'd probably be fetching more information about a given entity from a separate API endpoint, but we're just going to pull out the relevant employee object from the same data we use to populate the staff directory.

If a user is coming directly to a detail page, the list of employees won't yet be loaded, so we check the state and dispatch the *getEmployees* action if necessary.

We also need to add the mutation:

```
mutations: {
  // ...
  setSelectedEmployee(state, { employee }) {
    state.selectedEmployee = employee
  }
},
```

Within the *pages/users* folder, add the file *_id.vue* . Remember that beginning the name with an underscore lets Nuxt know this segment of the route will be dynamic.

**pages/users/_id.vue**

```
<template>
  <div
    v-if="selectedEmployee"
    class="ui main text container"
  >
    <div class="ui items">
      <div class="item">
        <div class="image">
          <img :src="selectedEmployee.picture.large">
        </div>
        <div class="content">
          <a class="header">{{ fullName }}</a>
          <div class="meta">
            <span>{{ selectedEmployee.email }}</span>
          </div>
          <div class="description">
            <p>
              {{ selectedEmployee.location.street }},
              {{ selectedEmployee.location.city }},
              {{ selectedEmployee.location.state }},
              {{ selectedEmployee.location.postcode }}
            </p>
          </div>
          <div class="extra">
            {{ selectedEmployee.phone }}<br>
            {{ selectedEmployee.cell }}
          </div>
        </div>
      </div>
```

```
        </div>
      </div>
    </div>
  </template>

  <script>
  import { mapState } from 'vuex'

  export default {
    fetch({ store, params }) {
      return store.dispatch('getEmployee', { id: params.id });
    },
    computed: {
      ...mapState(['selectedEmployee']),
      fullName() {
        return `${this.selectedEmployee.name.first} ${
          this.selectedEmployee.name.last
        }`;
      }
    }
  }
  </script>
```

The *fetch()* method gets the ID from the route parameters and dispatches the *getEmployee* action. As soon as the *selectedEmployee* state property is mutated, this change flows down to our page component and is rendered to the screen.

**aiden gray**

aiden.gray@example.com

3861 york road, lichfield, dyfed, SB8 3AR

01539 467142

0752-296-650

7-2. Details of an individual employee

## Creating the App Home Page

For the sake of completeness, we need to display something for the base route ( / ) of the app. Let's add a simple home screen.

**pages/index.vue**

```
<template>
  <div class="ui main text container">
    <h1 class="ui header">Chapter 7: Tying it all Together</h1>
    <p>This example builds upon everything we've covered in the book. It uses
    what we've learned to create a Nuxt.js app with a Vuex store and authentication,
    that fetches data from a remote API and displays it in a custom component,
    linking to a detail page for each item.</p>
    <p>Go to the <nuxt-link to="/users">Users page</nuxt-link>.</p>
  </div>
</template>
```

If you're editing the *index.vue* page generated by the Nuxt installer, be sure to delete the script and style blocks. They're no longer needed, and the CSS rules will conflict with our app styling.

By this point, you should have a functional application that loads a collection of employees' data from a remote API, and renders it using the StaffDirectory component. Clicking an employee should open a detail page with more information.

# Adding Authentication

Now that we have a basic Nuxt app up and running, let's take a look at how we might go about adding authentication.

Perhaps we want our basic staff directory to be available to all users, but to view the individual employee pages we'll require the user to log in.

The Nuxt community has developed a lot of third-party modules that add useful functionality to the framework quickly and easily. One such module is the <u>Nuxt</u>

Auth module[2], and we'll use this to add authentication to our app.

## Installing and Configuring the Auth Module

Installing the module is pretty straightforward via npm:

```
npm install @nuxtjs/auth
```

Once it's downloaded, we just need to tell Nuxt about it by editing the config file.

**nuxt.config.js**

```
// ...
modules: [
  '@nuxtjs/axios',
  '@nuxtjs/auth'
],
//...
```

The module provides us with some nice functionality that we'd otherwise have to spend time writing ourselves.

Once we provide some configuration regarding the authentication system we're using, it will handle logging in and out, provide convenience methods for checking the login state, and supply a middleware we can use to easily require authentication for pages and/or layouts.

As we're focused on the Nuxt side of things, we won't go into writing an authentication API here. Instead, we'll borrow the one that the Nuxt Auth module provides for its example.

---

2. https://auth.nuxtjs.org/

**Building an Authentication Back End**

If you're interested in writing your own auth server to use with a Nuxt app (or any kind of front-end JS app), SitePoint's article on <u>user authentication with the MEAN stack</u>[3] provides a solid starting point.

Create a new folder called `api` and copy the `auth.js` file from the <u>Nuxt community's auth-module GitHub repo</u>[4] into it.

We'll also need to install a couple of npm modules that this code depends on:

```
npm i cookie-parser express-jwt
```

The file sets up some Express-based API endpoints for logging in and out, and will authenticate any login with a non-empty username and a password of "123".

We need to tell Nuxt to include and run this file for us, by adding it to a `serverMiddleware` key in the config file:

```
serverMiddleware: ['~/api/auth'],
```

Also, we need to add some configuration to the file to tell the Auth module what strategy we want to use to authenticate:

```
auth: {
  strategies: {
    local: {
      endpoints: {
        login: { propertyName: 'token.accessToken' }
      }
    }
  }
},
```

---

[3.] https://www.sitepoint.com/user-authentication-mean-stack/
[4.] https://github.com/nuxt-community/auth-module/blob/dev/examples/api/auth.js

As with Nuxt itself, the Auth module comes with sensible conventions (which are also easy to change if you need to), so that's all we need to do here.

 **Authentication Strategies**

The Auth module provides a lot of flexibility to configure it to work with different authentications systems. The local strategy supports cookie and JWT systems.

There's also an OAuth strategy, and the module comes with several preconfigured "providers" for Google, Facebook, and GitHub authentication, among others. You can find out more in the Auth Module's Reference section[5].

## Adding the Login Page and Altering the Layout

One thing the module doesn't provide us with is a login page, so that's our next step. Create a component called *login.vue* inside the pages folder.

**pages/login.vue**

```
<template>
  <div class="ui main text container">
    <div class="ui middle aligned center aligned grid">
      <div class="column">
        <h2 class="ui green image header">
          <div class="content">
            Log in to your account
          </div>
        </h2>
        <form
          :class="{ error }"
          class="ui large form"
          @submit.prevent="onSubmit"
        >
          <div class="ui segment">
```

---

[5.] https://auth.nuxtjs.org/reference

```
            <div class="field">
              <div class="ui left icon input">
                <i class="user icon" />
                <input
                  v-model="username"
                  type="text"
                  placeholder="Username"
                >
              </div>
            </div>
            <div class="field">
              <div class="ui left icon input">
                <i class="lock icon" />
                <input
                  v-model="password"
                  type="password"
                  placeholder="Password"
                >
              </div>
            </div>
            <button
              type="submit"
              class="ui fluid large green submit button"
            >Login</button>
          </div>

          <div class="ui error message">Oops, we couldn't log you in!</div>

        </form>

      </div>
    </div>
  </div>
</template>

<script>
export default {
  data: () => ({
    username: '',
    password: '',
    error: null
  }),
  methods: {
```

```
    onSubmit() {
      this.$auth
        .loginWith('local', {
          data: {
            username: this.username,
            password: this.password
          }
        })
        .catch(e => {
          this.error = true
        });
    }
  }
}
</script>
```

This is almost identical to the login component we built previously, the main difference being in the `onSubmit()` method.

We take the username and password from the form, and pass them to the `login()` method of the Auth module, which is available inside our components as `this.$auth`.

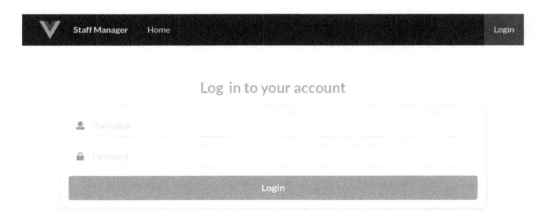

7-3. The app's login page

Let's also edit our layout template, to include a login/logout button, depending on the user's authentication status.

**layouts/default.vue**

```
<template>
  <div>
    <div class="ui fixed inverted menu">
      <div class="ui container">
        <a
          href="#"
          class="header item"
        >
          <img
            class="logo"
            src="~assets/logo.png"
          >
          Staff Manager
        </a>
        <nuxt-link
          class="item"
          to="/"
          exact
        >Home</nuxt-link>
        <nuxt-link
          class="item"
          to="/users"
        >Users</nuxt-link>
      </div>
      <div class="right menu">
        <a
          v-if="$auth.loggedIn"
          class="item"
          @click="$auth.logout()"
        >
          Logout
        </a>
        <nuxt-link
          v-else
          class="item"
          to="/login"
        >
          Login
```

```
      </nuxt-link>
    </div>
  </div>
  <nuxt/>
 </div>
</template>
```

The Auth module provides us with a nice  *loggedIn*  property to check if the current user has been authenticated, and a  *logout()*  method which will redirect the user back to the main route ( / ) by default.

The last thing we need to do is specify which pages require authentication to visit. We do this via a piece of middleware that the module provides for us.

Let's open up the employee detail page ( *_id.vue* ) and add it.

**pages/users/_id.vue**

```
export default {
  middleware: ['auth'],
  // ...
}
```

And with that, we should now have a authentication working for our app!

## Summary

Hopefully this chapter has helped to cement the things we learned about Nuxt, and to tie all of the topics you've learned together. The example app we made built upon concepts from almost every other chapter of the book.

We started by creating a new project with the Nuxt installer and setting up a Vuex store—utilizing knowledge of getters, mutations, and actions from <u>Chapter 5</u>. After building our own custom layout with the help of the Semantic UI CSS framework, we created pages to display a staff directory and employee details. Once the project was functional, we added in authentication with the help of the Auth module.